Questions People Ask in the Bible

Questions People Ask in the Bible

100 Meditations to Instruct and Inspire

by
Frank R. Shivers

Copyright 2025 by
Frank Shivers Evangelistic Association
All rights reserved
Printed in the United States of America

Unless otherwise noted, Scripture quotations are from
The Holy Bible *King James Version*

Library of Congress Cataloging-in-Publication Data

Shivers, Frank R., 1949-
Questions People Ask in the Bible / Frank Shivers
ISBN 978-1-878127-56-3

Library of Congress Control Number:
2024916510

Cover design by
Tim King

For Information:
Frank Shivers Evangelistic Association
2005 Congress Road
Hopkins, South Carolina 29061
www.frankshivers.com

Because
I have found Jesus to be everything He promised to be—
my Savior, Friend, Guide, Comforter, Helper, Teacher,
Shepherd, Sustainer, and much, much more—

I am excited to present this book to

_____

Date

_____

From

_____

with the prayer that reading its pages will enhance your walk with Jesus and be used by Him to minister to the needs and cares of your life.

Publications by Frank R. Shivers

"We are not writing upon water but carving upon imperishable material."[1]

– C. H. Spurgeon

The Preacher's Struggle and Stamina (Vol. 1)

The Preacher's Struggle and Stamina (Vol. 2)

Morning by Morning

Questions God Asks in the Bible

Questions People Ask in the Bible

The Widow's Comfort

When Things Just Don't Make Sense

When the Rain Comes

The Treasure of Grace

Persecuted for Christ's Sake

Basics of Biblical Praying

Christian Basics 101

Grief Beyond Measure, but Not Beyond Grace

Grief Beyond Measure, but Not Beyond Grace (Funeral Home Edition)

Growing Old, Honorably and Happily

The Wounded Spirit

The Wounded Spirit: Companion Workbook

Growing in Knowledge, Living by Faith

Marriage and Parenting Boosters

Caught Up to Heaven

Expositions of the Psalms (Three Volumes)

Life Principles from Proverbs

The Evangelism Apologetic Study Bible

Hot Buttons on Apologetics

Hot Buttons on Morality

Hot Buttons on Discipleship

The Pornography Trap

The Poison of Porn

Heavy Stuff

Heavy Stuff (Companion Workbook)

Clear Talk to Students

Nuggets of Truth (Three Volumes)

Soulwinning 101

Spurs to Soulwinning

Evangelistic Preaching 101

Evangelistic Praying

The Evangelistic Invitation 101

The Minister and the Funeral

Revivals 101

Children's Sermons that Connect

Be Careful Little Eyes

How to Preach Without Evangelistic Results (Pamphlet)

False Hopes of Heaven (Tract)

First Steps for New Believers (Tract)

The Goal Line Stand (Tract)

The Death Clock (Tract)

Scripture quotations taken from the Bible that are unmarked are from the King James Version.

Scriptures taken from the Holy Bible, New International Version®, NIV®. Copyright © 1973, 1978, 1984, 2011 by Biblica, Inc.™ Used by permission of Zondervan. All rights reserved worldwide. www.zondervan.com. The "NIV" and "New International Version" are trademarks registered in the United States Patent and Trademark Office by Biblica, Inc.™

Scripture quotations marked (NLT) are taken from the Holy Bible, New Living Translation, copyright ©1996, 2004, 2015 by Tyndale House Foundation. Used by permission of Tyndale House Publishers, Carol Stream, Illinois 60188. All rights reserved.

Scripture quotations marked (TLB) are taken from The Living Bible copyright © 1971. Used by permission of Tyndale House Publishers, Carol Stream, Illinois 60188. All rights reserved.

Scripture taken from the New Century Version®. Copyright © 2005 by Thomas Nelson. Used by permission. All rights reserved.

Scripture quotations taken from the Amplified® Bible (AMPC), Copyright © 1954, 1958, 1962, 1964, 1965, 1987 by The Lockman Foundation. Used by permission. www.lockman.org.

Scripture quotations taken from the Amplified® Bible (AMP), Copyright © 2015 by The Lockman Foundation. Used by permission. www.lockman.org.

Quotations marked ESV are taken from the ESV, (The Holy Bible, English Standard Version), copyright 2001 by Crossway, a publishing ministry of Good News Publishers. Used by permission.

"The Lord shines upon us in the question."[2]
– C. H. Spurgeon

To

Joseph A. Clayton

In June 1974, upon graduating from seminary and entering vocational evangelism, I ministered in my first revival as an evangelist at Pine Grove Baptist Church, Sumter, South Carolina, with pastor Joe Clayton. (I worked with him as a seminary student at Stedman Baptist Church, Leesville, South Carolina.) Joe and his wife, Jennie Rae (now in Heaven), immediately became partners in my ministry, helping where needed. They were Aquila and Priscilla to me. Joe served on the Board of Directors and played a considerable role in developing our revival and camp ministry. Jennie Rae served as ministry secretary and, with Joe, worked sacrificially in our summer camp program.

Joe's devotion to the Lord, strong, bold faith, intense prayer life, and encouragement have bolstered me and my evangelistic work for nearly fifty-five years.

"A sudden bold and unexpected question does many times surprise a man and lay him open."

– Francis Bacon.

Contents

Preface

1. Mordecai asked: "Who knoweth whether thou art come to the kingdom for such a time as this?"
2. David asked: "How shall a young man cleanse his way?"
3. Jeremiah asked: "Is there no balm in Gilead?"
4. Paul asked: "Shall we sin because we are not under the law, but under grace?"
5. The Hebrews author asked: "How shall we escape if we neglect so great a salvation?"
6. Nehemiah asked: "Why is the house of God forsaken?"
7. Paul asked: "Are you really Christians?"
8. Paul asked: "How say some among you that there is no resurrection of the dead?"
9. James asked: "For what is your life?"
10. The Jailer asked: "Sirs, what must I do to be saved?"
11. Paul asked: "Who hindered you, that ye should not obey the truth?"
12. David asked: "Why art thou cast down, O my soul?"
13. David asked: "What is man?"
14. Elihu asked: "Where is God my Maker?"
15. Elihu asked: "Where is God my Maker, who giveth songs in the night?"
16. The Israelites asked: "Can God furnish a table in the wilderness?"
17. The Israelites asked: "How shall we sing the Lord's song in a strange land?"
18. Solomon asked: "Who hath woe? Who hath sorrow?"
19. Nehemiah asked: "Why should the work cease?"
20. Paul asked: "For if the trumpet give an uncertain sound, who shall prepare himself to the battle?"

21. Eliphaz asked: "Are the consolations of God small with thee?"
22. A Lawyer asked: "Who is my neighbor?"
23. The Rich Young Ruler asked: "What shall I do that I may inherit eternal life?"
24. Belshazzar asked: "Are you the Daniel brought from Israel as a captive by King Nebuchadnezzar?"
25. Elisha asked: "Where fell it?"
26. David asked: "If the foundations be destroyed, what can the righteous do?"
27. Solomon asked: "A wounded spirit who can bear?"
28. Paul asked: "Know ye not that those who run in a race all run, but one receiveth the prize?"
29. Job asked: "What profit should we have if we pray unto Him?"
30. Pilate asked: "What will you do with Jesus?"
31. Amos asked: "Can two walk together unless they be agreed?"
32. Job asked: "Shall vain words [words that fail to comfort] have an end?"
33. Simon Peter asked: "Lord, to whom shall we go?"
34. David asked: "And now, Lord, what wait I for?"
35. Paul asked: "Lord, what wilt Thou have me to do?"
36. The Disciples asked: "Why could not we cast him out?"
37. The Disciples asked: "Who then can be saved?"
38. The People asked: "Who is this son of man?"
39. Malachi asked: "Who can endure the day of his coming?"
40. Moses asked: "What doth the Lord thy God require of thee?"
41. David asked: "Wherewithal shall a young man cleanse his way?"
42. Gehazi asked: "Is it well with you?"

43. Phillip asked: "Understandest thou what thou readest?"
44. Scoffers asked: "Where is the promise of his coming?"
45. Paul asked: "O death, where is thy sting?"
46. Paul asked: "Who shall separate us from the love of Christ?"
47. The Samaritan woman asked: "From whence then hast thou that living water?"
48. James asked: "Is any sick among you?"
49. Martha asked: "Dost thou not care that my sister hath left me to serve alone?"
50. Moses asked: "Who is on the Lord's side?"
51. Joshua asked: "What mean these stones?"
52. The Disciples asked: "What shall be the sign of thy coming?"
53. Gideon asked: "With what shall I save Israel?"
54. David asked: "Is the child dead?"
55. Absalom asked: "Is this thy kindness to thy friend?"
56. Thomas asked: "How can we know the way?"
57. Paul asked: "And how shall they preach, except they be sent?"
58. The Daughters of Jerusalem asked: "What is thy beloved more than another beloved?"
59. Paul asked: "What is our crown of rejoicing?"
60. The Psalmist asked: "Wilt thou not revive us again?"
61. Solomon asked: "Do you see a man who is hasty in his words?"
62. David asked: "Put my tears in Your bottle. Are they not in Your book?"
63. Ethan the Ezrahite asked: "What man is he that liveth, and shall not see death?"

64. Solomon asked: "Who hath ascended up into heaven, or descended?"

65. King Lemuel's mother asked: "Who can find a virtuous woman?"
66. Ezekiel asked: "Should not the shepherds feed the flocks?"
67. The Sadducees asked: "In the resurrection, therefore, when they shall rise, whose wife shall she be of them?"
68. The Pharisees asked: "Is it lawful for a man to put away his wife for every cause?"
69. James asked: "What causes quarrels, and what causes fights among you?"
70. Paul asked: "Know ye not that a little leaven leaveneth the whole lump?"
71. The Israelites asked: "What trespass is this that ye have committed against the God of Israel?"
72. David asked: "What shall be done to the man that killeth this Philistine?"
73. David asked: "Is there not a cause?"
74. Isaiah asked: "And he said, "What shall I cry?"
75. Judas asked: "Why was not this ointment sold for three hundred pence, and given to the poor?"
76. The angels asked: "Why stand ye gazing up into heaven?"
77. The author of Hebrews asked: "Are they not all ministering spirits?"
78. The Eunuch asked: "What doth hinder me to be baptized?"
79. David asked: "What is man?"
80. Peter asked: "Why has Satan filled your heart to lie to the Holy Spirit?"
81. Jeremiah asked: "Why do the wicked prosper?"
82. David asked: "Whom shall I fear?"
83. David asked: "Wilt not thou deliver my feet from falling?"
84. Solomon asked: "Who is able to stand before envy?"

85. Solomon asked: "Can a man take fire in his bosom, and his clothes not be burned?"
86. Solomon asked: "Who can say, I have made my heart clean, I am pure from my sin?"
87. Isaiah asked: "Who hath believed our report?"
88. A scribe asked: "Which is the first commandment of all?"
89. Paul asked: "What fellowship hath righteousness with unrighteousness?"
90. Micah asked: "What doth the Lord require of thee?"
91. Paul asked: "If the foot shall say, Because I am not the hand, I am not of the body; is it therefore not of the body?"
92. Paul asked: "Do I seek to please men?"
93. David asked: "Why standest Thou afar off, O Lord?"
94. The four lepers asked: "Why sit we here until we die?"
95. Job asked: "And where is now my hope?"
96. Ahab asked: "Art thou he that troubleth Israel?"
97. Moses asked: "Shall your brethren go to war, and shall ye sit here?"
98. Jeremiah asked: "What will you do when the end comes?"
99. Paul asked: "What? know ye not that your body is the temple of the Holy Ghost?"
100. Paul asked: "How are the dead raised up? And with what body do they come?"

Preface

The Bible contains 3,298 questions, 1,024 in the New Testament, and 2,274 in the Old Testament.[3] Making them and their answers adaptable to all is the work of the Holy Spirit.

Spurgeon asserts, "No Scripture is of private interpretation: no text has spent itself upon the person who first received it. God's comforts are like wells, which no one man or set of men can drain dry; however, mighty may be their thirst. A well may be opened for Hagar, but that well is never closed, and any other wanderer may drink at it."[4] With that in mind, put yourself in the shoes of a question's original recipient and claim it and its answer personally for the enrichment and edification of your soul.

Questions People Ask in the Bible and its companion, *Questions God Asks in the Bible*, contain 100 questions and answers each, ideal for devotionals, small group study, and sermons.

1

Mordecai asked: "Who knoweth whether thou art come to the kingdom for such a time as this?"

"Who knoweth whether thou art come to the kingdom for such a time as this?" (Esther 4:14). Mordecai was right. God had put Esther in the palace to thwart Haman's holocaust of the Jews. It was the great opportunity of her lifetime, perhaps the reason for her birth. Fortunately, she rose to the life-jeopardizing challenge of interceding for the people to the king, and they were saved (Esther 4:15–16).

Throughout life, sometimes suddenly and fleetingly, divine appointments arise to use one's gifts, talents, position, wealth, and popularity to intervene on God's behalf against the tidal waves of evil. As Esther's case shows us, redeeming them takes concern, compulsion, and courage—and sometimes, the challenge from Mordecai. Note eight pivotal lessons.

1. A reason must be searched out for why "thou art come to the kingdom for such a time as this." "Who knoweth?" to what purpose has the Lord placed you where you are positionally at this particular time?

2. The danger looms of doing nothing in the face of evil when divinely positioned to make a difference ("For if thou altogether holdest thy peace at this time").

3. It is a severe sin (one of omission) not to stand when we ought to stand. Matthew Henry says, "We should every one of us consider for what end God has put us in the place where we are and study to answer that end; and, when any particular opportunity of serving God and our generation offers itself, we must take care that we do not let it slip, for we were entrusted with it that we might improve it."

4. God's judgment will fall on the man who falters on the day of opportunity.

5. God will use another to do what we will not do ("deliverance [will] arise to the Jews from another place").

6. Fear is overcome by faith. The man who does God's bidding is not without God's presence and power. "Thou needest not fear miscarrying in the enterprise; if God designed thee for it, He will bear thee out and give thee success."

7. Prayer and fasting thwart the plans of the wicked (Mark 9:29).

8. One must, at times, risk life and limb for the Divine call. Esther's going before the king uncalled placed her life in jeopardy.

"If God has a purpose to serve by a man, that man will live out his day and accomplish the Divine design."[5]—C. H. Spurgeon.

2
David asked: "How shall a young man cleanse his way?"

"How shall a young man cleanse his way?" (Psalm 119:9 KJ21). The question means, "Wherewithal shall a young man purge himself of sinful defilement and walk in holiness as a saint?" There is one moral guide to govern life honorably and successfully—the word of God (Psalm 119:10). It is plain, unchanging, inerrant, and applicable to all. Gill states, "The word of God is a most powerful antidote against sin, when it has a place in the heart; not only the precepts of it forbid sin, but the promises of it influence and engage to the purity of heart and life."[6]

No person can go wrong navigating life with the Bible as his guide, chart, and compass. The Word prevents sin, points out sin, purges sin, purifies from sin, and protects from sin's powerful consequences. It is the cleanest "Book" and will enable all who embrace its truth to be clean fully. "Sanctify them through thy truth: thy word is truth" (John 17:17). The man who rules his life by God's Word will be found to be honest, holy, happy, religious, reverent, and triumphant (Joshua 1:8; Psalm 1:3).

Spurgeon advises, "Let each man, who desires to be holy, have a holy watchfulness in his heart, and keep his Holy Bible before his open eye. There, he will find every turn of the road marked down, every slough and miry place pointed out, with the way to go through unsoiled; and there, too, he will find light for his darkness, comfort for his weariness, and company for his loneliness."[7]

Matthew Henry similarly counsels, "The ruin of young men is either living at large (or by no rule at all) or choosing to themselves false rules. Let them ponder the path of their feet, and walk by Scripture rules; so their way shall be clean, and they shall have the comfort and credit of it here and forever."[8] Deviation from the pure and clean path (there are multiplied people and manifold pleasures that seek to turn us from the path) to that of moral filthiness occurs when a person fails "to take heed" to such godly instruction. See Philippians 2:13.

David hides God's Word in his heart to conquer sin's temptation. "Not merely in his memory, not in the intellectual powers of the mind, but in the city and citadel, where the affections dwell, where reason governs, the home of motive, of principle, and feeling. The memory should be the storehouse of the Divine truth; it is often the very quiver of God, from which He draws His arrows of conviction and the storehouse where He draws comfort and peace for His people."[9]

Say with David, "I will delight myself in thy statutes; I will not forget thy word" (Psalm 119:16 KJ21). Though unseen, the Word of God in the coffin of his heart "constituted the secret power by which he was governed; it was permanently deposited there, as the most valuable of his treasures."[10] Spurgeon said, "The Bible in the memory is better than the Bible in the bookcase."

"A guide of conduct must be decisive, and there is no faltering in the utterance of the Book as to right and wrong."—Alexander Maclaren.

3

Jeremiah asked: "Is there no balm in Gilead?"

"Is there no balm in Gilead? Is there no physician there?" (Jeremiah 8:22 ASV). The balm of Gilead, though costly, was a highly effective medicine to treat wounds. It could be obtained in

Gilead (a former region in modern-day Jordan). In a time when physicians were rarely successful (based on texts like Job 13:4 and 2 Chronicles 16:12–13), doctors in Gilead were, probably because they confined themselves to balsam medicine.[11]

The questions of Jeremiah stand as a rebuke to Israel's persistent backsliding and stubbornness in not seeking its available cure. Out of a broken heart for them, despite their pollution and defilement, the prophet cried, "Oh that my head were waters, and mine eyes a fountain of tears, that I might weep day and night for the slain of the daughter of my people!" (Jeremiah 9:1).

The metaphor presents Christ as the Great Physician who possesses healing medicine (the balm of His blood and His Word) for the diseased and ravaged soul. Simeon states, "Has not God sent us a Physician from Heaven, even His only dear Son, who perfectly knows the extent of our disorders and is able to prescribe a remedy for them? Other physicians find their remedies in the productions of nature and of art, but this blessed Physician 'heals His people with His own stripes.' He shed His precious blood for us upon the cross that it might be applied, as a sovereign balm, to our souls to restore us to perfect health."

The Bible says, "The blood of Jesus Christ His Son cleanseth us from all sin" (1 John 1:7). "He [Christ] is the only universal doctor," Spurgeon writes, "and the medicine He gives is the only true catholicon [a cure-all], healing in every instance. Whatever our spiritual malady, we should immediately apply to this Divine Physician. There is no brokenness of heart which Jesus cannot bind up. We have but to think of the myriads who have been delivered from all sorts of diseases through the power and virtue of His touch, and we shall joyfully put ourselves in His hands. We trust Him, and sin dies; we love Him, and grace lives; we wait for Him, and grace is strengthened; we see Him as He is, and grace is perfected forever."

The psalmist declared, "He healeth the broken in heart, and bindeth up their wounds" (Psalm 147:3)—and "what He's done for others, He'll do for you." *The physician is in* and awaits your request for His soothing and healing balm for whatever the ailment might be.

"Christ is the Good Physician. There is no disease He cannot heal, no sin He cannot remove, no trouble He cannot help. He is the Balm of Gilead, the Great Physician who has never yet failed to heal all the spiritual maladies of every soul that has come unto Him in faith and prayer."—James H. Aughey.

4

Paul asked: "Shall we sin because we are not under the law, but under grace?"

"Shall we sin because we are not under the law, but under grace?" (Romans 6:15 KJ21).

Paul debunked the belief that since grace covers all our sins, we can sin all we want. In Romans 6:15, he said, "What then? Shall we sin [deliberative sin], because we are not under the law [Mosaic law], but under grace [forgiveness of sin at the Cross]? God forbid" (Clarke says the Greek word means, "Let it not be, far from it, by no means."[12]). Paul is making clear that it is egregiously wrong to equate grace with liberty to sin, that is, that grace is not a license to sin all you want. Christ died upon the Cross to forgive man of sin, not enable him in it. The evidence that a man has experienced grace is manifested in his desire to avoid sin, not seek it (1 John 3:4–10). The bottom line is that the Gospel (grace) does not allow a man to sin any more than the Mosaic law's statutes, commandments, and regulations. Therefore, be careful to use grace rightfully and not abuse it through a heretical presumptuousness that sanctions a lifestyle of licentiousness and wantonness. See Hebrews 10:26.

R. M. Edgar says, "The liberty *grace* gives is totally distinct from license. License is the liberty to please ourselves, to humor the flesh, and to regard liberty as an end and not a means. But God, in His Gospel, gives no such liberty. His liberty is a means and not an end; it is liberty to live as He pleases, liberty to love Him and love men, liberty to serve one another by love. We must guard ourselves, then, from the confusion of mistaking license for liberty."[13] Barnes says, "It is needful to guard the doctrine of grace [the freedom it renders] from abuse at all times. There has been a strong tendency, as the history of the church has shown, to abuse the doctrine of grace."[14]

Christians have engaged in gross acts of immorality and other wicked indulgences due to a ludicrous and perverted view of gospel liberty. The Bible makes crystal clear that "Christ came to call sinners to repentance, not to licentiousness; to take His yoke upon them, and yield their members instruments of righteousness unto holiness"[15] (Romans 6:13). Peter says similarly, "You are free from the law, but that doesn't mean you are free to do wrong. Live as those who are free to do only God's will at all times" (1 Peter 2:16 TLB).

MacArthur explains, "The freedom Christians have is not a base from which they can sin freely and without consequence."[16] MacDonald agrees, saying, "The Christian's freedom is in Christ Jesus (Galatians 2:4), and this excludes any possible thought that it might ever mean freedom to sin."[17] Matthew Henry says, "The Gospel is a doctrine according to godliness (1 Timothy 6:3), and is so far from giving the least countenance to sin, that it lays us under the strongest obligation to avoid and subdue it."[18] See Romans 6:1–4. McGee states, "What does the Gospel of grace do for the believer? It is grace, not law, that frees us from doing wrong and allows us to do right. Grace does not set us free *to* sin, but it sets us free *from* sin."[19]

The freedom that grace grants the believer is not purposed to allow the indulgence of sinful and corrupt passions but to enable a life of righteousness and holiness. But by what means is moral restraint to be bestowed? Not by the law, but by the indwelling and controlling ministry of the Holy Spirit (2 Thessalonians 2:7). "Walk in the Spirit, and ye shall not fulfill the lust of the flesh" (Galatians 5:16). See Galatians 2:21.

> What, then! Shall Christians sin,
>   Because freed from the law?
> Shall sinners, saved by grace divine,
>   From holiness withdraw?

Shall grace seduce the mind,
    And lead the soul astray?
And souls who under grace are found,
    Delight to disobey?

Great God, forbid the thought!
    Preserve thy saints in love.
While Pharisees set grace at naught,
    Saints shall thy ways approve.

– William Gadsby (1844)

"A true Christian does not see God's promise of forgiveness as a license to sin, a way to abuse His love and presume on His grace. Rather, he sees God's gracious forgiveness as the means to spiritual growth and sanctification."[20]—John MacArthur.

5

The Hebrews author asked: "How shall we escape if we neglect so great a salvation?"

"How shall we escape, if we neglect so great salvation?" (Hebrews 2:3). The author states that since Jesus is superior to the Law and the angels because He is the Son of God and alone provides salvation, they (non-Christians) must not drift away from acceptance and submission to Him, for if they do, 'how shall they escape' the eternal punishment to come?

The salvation God provides is great.

It is great because of its benefits. Its recipient gains justification from sin (1 Corinthians 6:11). Its recipient gains reconciliation with God (Romans 5:10). Its recipient gains liberation from sin (Romans 6:6, 14). Its recipient gains reservation for Heaven (Psalm 16:11). Believers are saved from Hell and its torments and given access to the City of God at death.

It is great because of its means. "The law of Moses was unable to save us because of the weakness of our sinful nature. So God did what the law could not do. He sent his own Son in a body like the bodies we sinners have. And in that body God declared an end to sin's control over us by giving his Son as a sacrifice for our sins" (Romans 8:3 NLT). Jesus made a bridge to God for man out of the timber of the Cross. Salvation is a great salvation because of the great cost of providing it—the torturous death of the Son of God on a cruel cross (John 3:16; 2 Timothy 1:10).

It is great because of its availability. Salvation is every man's privilege and possibility. All who will be saved may be saved, "even me with all my sin." It's not a white man's salvation. It's not a black man's salvation. It's the world's salvation. None are excluded, regardless of face, race or place. It is a great salvation for great sinners.

How shall you escape if you *neglect* this so great a salvation? How shall you escape a wasted and ill-spent life? How shall you escape a wasted and wanton influence? How shall you escape drifting further from Christ? How shall you escape the consequences of sin? How shall you escape Hell? The question is unanswerable, for there is no way of escape from these things apart from the blood of Jesus Christ shed at Calvary for the remission of man's sin.

"To live one hour apart from Christ is to live in infinite peril, since in that hour you may die and pass beyond the realms of hope."[21]—C. H. Spurgeon.

6

Nehemiah asked: "Why is the house of God forsaken?"

"Why is the house of God forsaken?" (Nehemiah 13:11). Nehemiah asked this question when the house of God and the holy things of God were being neglected and forsaken. It's a relevant question today.

Why is the house of God forsaken?

1. The church declines because of being displaced by virtual worship. Virtual worship can never replace the need for what in-house worship affords (Hebrews 10:25).

2. It declines because of discord among the members. Members and outsiders alike are repelled by the faction, fussing, and feuding witnessed within the church's doors.

3. It declines because of departure from the Bible being preached and taught soundly as the authoritative Word of God (Proverbs 29:18). The power and blessing of God are withheld from the church, which minimizes the Word of God (1 Corinthians 2:4).

4. It declines because its services are dull, fueled by cold formality and ritualism. The church becomes a valley of dry bones when the Holy Spirit's fire is quenched.

5. It declines because of the negative impression among the unsaved due to inconsistent churchgoers (Leviticus 19:14). Hypocritical behavior turns the unsaved away from the church.

6. It declines because of a funding deficit (Haggai 1:4). Financial struggles force church closures.

7. It declines because of a disconnect between the pulpit and the pew (Jeremiah 3:15). Preaching and teaching that fail to connect with the needs of the man in the pew discourage attendance.

8. It declines because of a lack of desire by members to attend (Psalm 122:1). Aughey rightly says, "A little thing will keep them from the house of God who has no desire to go to it."

9. It declines primarily because of the darkness that encompasses the unregenerate, blinding them to the need of Christ and, therefore, His church (2 Corinthians 4:4; 2 Timothy 3:1–5).

"Churches should evaluate everything they do to determine how it can be done better."—Thom S. Rainer.

7

Paul asked: "Are you really Christians?"

"Are you really Christians? Do you pass the test? Do you feel Christ's presence and power more and more within you? Or are you just pretending to be Christians when actually you aren't at all?"

(2 Corinthians 13:5 TLB). Gill says, "The name of Christ was named upon them in their baptism; Christ had been preached to them. This the apostle knew; but all this might be, and yet Christ not dwell in their hearts by faith. This is the great point the apostle directs them to examine and prove themselves about, whether Christ was in them by a lively faith?"[22]

Note:

1. The person of the test. The "believer" is instructed to make sure his salvation is genuine, not a counterfeit.

2. The purpose of the test. An examination is needful, for among the wheat in the church are tares (Matthew 13:24–30). One may teach like Nicodemus, be devoted to his religion like Saul of Tarsus, be baptized like Simon Magus, and be a respected and trusted officer among the saints (church) like Judas (disciple band) and still miss Heaven. Unto all who are religious but not reborn, Jesus will say at the Judgment, "I never knew you." Make sure of salvation. Watchman Nee said, "There is nothing more tragic than to come to the end of life and know we have been on the wrong course."

3. The procedure of the test. To obtain assurance of salvation, Paul says to "prove yourselves." Assurance is obtainable and knowable. Question your heart inside and out to determine whether it is genuine or counterfeit based upon the Word of God. Did you repent of sin and exhibit faith in Jesus Christ as Lord and Savior (Acts 20:21)? Does a change in conduct back up that *experience* as genuine (2 Corinthians 5:17)? Implore the Holy Spirit for His help and verdict (Romans 8:16). Be truthful and thorough, for a mistake in examining and proving salvation cannot be rectified upon death.

4. The profit of the test. Examination of one's faith is beneficial all the way around, for it confirms the authenticity and genuineness of faith, enabling the believer to say earnestly, "I know whom I have believed, and am persuaded that he is able to keep that which I have committed unto him" (2 Timothy 1:12), or it reveals a false hope and enables him to embrace genuine salvation through repentance and faith.

"Questions and doubts be heard no more; let Christ and joy be all our theme. His Spirit seals his Gospel sure, to every soul that trusts in him."—Isaac Watts (1744).

8

Paul asked: "How say some among you that there is no resurrection of the dead?"

"How say some among you that there is no resurrection of the dead?" (1 Corinthians 15:12).

In 1 Corinthians, Paul argues the absurdity of denying the resurrection of Christ by stating eight things that denial would mean.

1. If Christ was not raised from the dead, it would mean He is still in the tomb (1 Corinthians 15:13). This is absurd given the "many infallible proofs" (Acts 1:3) that substantiate that it is empty due to His resurrection. The case for Christ's resurrection has over five hundred eyewitnesses, including both believers and unbelievers (1 Corinthians 15:6).

2. If Christ were not raised, it would mean the Christian faith is a delusion and is, therefore, ineffective and worthless (1 Corinthians 15:14b). The proof of Jesus' deity and Messiahship lies in His resurrection.

3. If Christ was not raised, our preaching would be futile (1 Corinthians 15:14a). Knowledgeable preachers and theologians have proclaimed the resurrection in thousands of pulpits. If Christ had not been raised, all their preaching would have been for naught, as would be ours today.

4. If Christ was not raised, then sin retains its destructive and damning power (1 Corinthians 15:17).[23] The resurrection enables the believer to say, "O death, where is thy sting? O grave, where is thy victory? The sting of death is sin; and the strength of sin is the law. But thanks be to God, which giveth us the victory through our Lord Jesus Christ" (1 Corinthians 15:55–57).

5. If Christ was not raised, then all who maintain His resurrection are liars (1 Corinthians 15:15). Paul puts his veracity, that of all the apostles and every other Christian, on the line to substantiate the fact of Christ's resurrection.

6. If Christ were not raised, then the believers' faith is vain, and they are hopelessly lost (1 Corinthians 15:17b). Apart from the resurrection, there is no remission of sin and, therefore, no salvation (Romans 10:9–13). Christ's resurrection puts God's divine seal upon what He did on Good Friday to atone for man's sin, showing that it was acceptable and efficacious.

7. If Christ were not raised, there would be no reunion with loved ones in Heaven (1 Corinthians 15:18). Pratt says, "If faith were in vain, then every Christian who had died would never receive an eternal benefit for having repented and believed. All who had died in Christ would never realize any part of the salvation for which they hoped; everything would have been a lie."[24]

8. If Christ were not raised, it would mean that Christians are the most miserable of all men (1 Corinthians 15:19). New Testament Christians, for the sake of Christ, sacrifice friends, family, comfort, jobs, fame, and at times, their lives. Thus, if the cherished hope of Christ's resurrection were false, voiding the value and benefit of their sacrifices and service, they, of all people, would be bitterly disappointed.

Paul closes the argument by saying emphatically, "But Christ has indeed been raised from the dead" (1 Corinthians 15:20 NIV). And because He has risen, all the absurd propositions Paul suggested are reversed. God raised "Jesus our Lord from the dead. He was handed over to die because of our sins, and he was raised to life to make us right with God" (Romans 4:24–25 NLT). "The God of our fathers raised up Jesus, whom you put to death by hanging Him on a cross. He is the one whom God exalted to His right hand as a Prince and a Savior, to grant repentance to Israel, and forgiveness of sins" (Acts 5:30–31 NASB).

"Take away the resurrection," Paul said, "and you destroy both the foundation and the fabric of the Christian faith."[25]—William Barclay.

9

James asked: "For what is your life?"

"Whereas ye know not what shall be on the morrow. For what is your life? It is even a vapour, that appeareth for a little time, and then vanisheth away" (James 4:14). James' question warns against presumptuous confidence in the continuance of our life tomorrow.[26] He says life is a mere "vapor" that vanishes quickly. The word "vapor" used in comparison to life is common in the Scriptures.[27] It means "a mist, an exhalation, a smoke; such a vapor as we see ascending from a stream, or as lies on the mountainside on the morning, or as floats for a little time in the air, but which is dissipated by the rising sun, leaving not a trace behind."[28] Note, "Like a puff of smoke or a wisp of steam from a cooking pot" (James 4:14 AMP), we soon vanish from this life.

In Psalm 90, Moses likens man's lifetime to seven things:

1. A speck of a day.

2. Changing the guards at specific intervals during the night watches (which only last a portion of the night).

3. A dream that quickly disappears.

4. A blade of grass that "grows up" in the morning into full blossom only to wither and die in the evening. Spurgeon says, "As grass is green in the morning and hay at night, so people are changed from health to corruption in a few hours."

5. Like "a tale that is told." Perowne says a tale refers to "a brief passing utterance" or "fleeting sound."

6. A mighty gale-force wind that blows chaff or straw away, here now but swept away quickly.

7. A bird that "flies away." At man's first breath, man swiftly flies toward death.[29]

Shakespeare said, "Out, out, brief candle! Life's but a walking shadow." The hands on the clock or watch, the passing of one day to the next, the throbbing beat of the heart, the sudden death of others, and the growing decay of the body all testify to life's frailty, brevity, and uncertainty.

As the parade roared down the avenue, Caesar's Praetorian Guard whispered to him, "Remember, Caesar, thou art mortal."[30] Personalize and preach those words to yourself until they are believed and acted upon.

Matthew Henry asserts, "It is an excellent art rightly to number our days so as not to be out in our calculation. We must live under a constant apprehension of the shortness and uncertainty of life and the near approach of death and eternity."[31] Pray, "Lord, make me to know mine end, and the measure of my days, what it is: that I may know how frail I am" (Psalm 39:4) that I "may develop inner wisdom" (Psalm 90:12 ISV) as how best to live.

In light of life's transitoriness, James instructs us never to make plans and commitments for tomorrow without the addendum "if the Lord wills" (James 4:15).

"All men think all men are mortal, but themselves."—Edward Young.

10

The Jailer asked: "Sirs, what must I do to be saved?"

"Sirs, what must I do to be saved?" (Acts 16:30). The question of the Philippian jailer to Paul and Silas is every man's pressing question. Why ask it?

1. Because its answer brings an escape from who you are. Man cannot fix his despair and misery, emptiness and hopelessness, brokenness and shamefulness, and shackles and chains of addiction

by himself. But Jesus Christ can and does that for everyone who turns to Him in faith for help and healing (Romans 10:13). He transforms man from the inside out (2 Corinthians 5:17). What man needs to be different is not human resolution but divine regeneration, the new birth (John 3:3).

2. Because its answer brings entry into what you need. Jesus says, "I am the door: by me if any man enter in, he shall be saved, and shall go in and out, and find pasture" (John 10:9). Outside the door of salvation is a form of Hell on earth, but inside it is a taste of Heaven and all that is needed to fill the empty soul. You can enter this door by exhibiting a belief in who Jesus is and what He did to make possible the forgiveness of sin, and acting upon that belief by coming to Him in faith and repentance (turning from sin). In finding Jesus, man finds sufficiency for every need (John 10:10; 2 Corinthians 3:5).

3. Because its answer brings peace to how and where you will go at death. Will your deathbed be serene, peaceful, full of hope and assurance of a future life in Heaven, or wrought with terror, trembling, and anxiety over the prospect of Hell? To live hopefully and happily and die peacefully with the assurance of Heaven, a person must ask the jailer's question and take its answer.

"Those who are thoroughly convinced of sin and truly concerned about their salvation will give themselves up to Christ."—Matthew Henry.

11

Paul asked: "Who hindered you, that ye should not obey the truth?"

"Who hindered you, that ye should not obey the truth?" (Galatians 5:7 KJ21). Bondage to the law caused some Galatian believers to stumble in the faith. Hindrances of all sorts cause the Christian runner to stumble and falter as he competes for the crown of the high calling of God in Christ Jesus.

The question is pressed to you, who have stumbled and faltered in the race. What hindered you?

1. Was it religious surfing? The search among heretical faiths ("whoring after other gods"—Judges 2:17) for something better than the truth embraced brings spiritual collapse.

2. Was it past spiritual highs? Spiritual and emotional highs experienced at conversion, summer camp, or revival are fleeting. You can't live on them—it can't be done. A daily fresh encounter with God is imperative for spiritual progress (Matthew 17:4; John 15:5).

3. Was it disillusionment? Bitter disappointment can come from tethering oneself to a church, teacher, preacher, or ministry instead of Christ and His Word (Jeremiah 17:5; Psalm 111:8–9). Man disappoints, but Christ doesn't.

4. Was it a bitter disappointment? Animosity toward God for not answering prayer as requested and permitting sorrow, sickness, and suffering undermines and jeopardizes the believer's faith. Spurgeon says, "The worldling blesses God while He gives him plenty, but the Christian blesses him when He smites him: he believes Him to be too wise to err and too good to be unkind; he trusts Him where he cannot trace him, looks up to Him in the darkest hour, and believes that all is well."[32]

5. Was it a secret sin? Failure to "lay aside…the sin which doth so easily beset us" will eventually slay us (Hebrews 12:1). Sin suffocates the sacred, stagnates the soul, and stunts spiritual growth. Paul cautions, "A little leaven leaveneth the whole lump" (Galatians 5:9). And Solomon tells us to guard against "the little foxes, that spoil the vines" (Song of Solomon 2:15).

6. Was it distractions? School, sports, work, relationships, and pleasures are potential distractions in living for Jesus. Demas failed to handle distractions successfully and drifted from his first love for Christ (2 Timothy 4:10; 2 Timothy 3:4). Don't allow worldly stuff to crowd out time for church, communion with God, Bible study, and Christian service (Luke 9:56–62).

7. Was it presumptuous complacency? Havner wrote, "Comfort precedes collapse."

8. Was it the wrong companions? Many believers, predominantly the youthful, are hindered in the Christian walk by friends' corrupting example and influence. "He that walketh with wise men shall be wise: but a companion of fools shall be destroyed" (Proverbs 13:20). "And have *no fellowship* with the unfruitful works of darkness, but rather reprove them" (Ephesians 5:11). A person takes on the *image and lifestyle* of him with which he associates.

A Dutch proverb says, "He that lives with cripples learns to limp," and the Spanish say, "He that goes with wolves learns to howl." To be wise, associate with the wise. A man's friends can be his most helpful allies or most destructive enemies. "Tell me with whom you walk, and I will tell you who you are" (Spanish proverb).

Where did you stumble? Return to the place with contrition of heart and be restored. "So now, correct your ways and deeds, and obey the Lord your God" (Jeremiah 26:13 CSB). The race doesn't belong to the swift but to him that keeps running.

"Everything that can influence the present temper and future state of the soul is weighty and important."[33]—J. Orton.

12

David asked: "Why art thou cast down, O my soul?"

"Why art thou cast down, O my soul?" (Psalm 42:5). "David," says Calvin, "represents himself here as divided into two parts. In so far as he rests through faith in God's promises, he raises himself, equipped with the spirit of an invincible valor against the feelings of the flesh, and at the same time blames his weakness."[34]

What to do when down in the dumps of despair?

1. Talk yourself out of it. David did (Psalm 43:5). Trapp says, "David chideth David out of the dumps."[35] In times of deepest distraught when the heart is bleeding profusely (Psalm 77:2), sleep is elusive (Psalm 77:4), and comfort is not to be found, talk to God; then speak to yourself (Psalm 42:5). Verbalize the doubts and then allow faith to answer based upon the God of history, the Bible and the mercies of God experienced by others and yourself.

Boice states, "It is a case of the mind speaking to the emotions rather than the emotions dictating to the mind."[36] D. Martyn Lloyd-Jones said in the time of despair, "You have to take yourself in hand; you have to address yourself, preach to yourself, question yourself. You must say to your soul: 'Why art thou cast down—what business have you to be disquieted?' You must turn on yourself, upbraid yourself, condemn yourself, encourage yourself, and say to yourself: 'Hope thou in God'—instead of muttering in this depressed, unhappy way."[37]

2. Talk to yourself, like David, commanding your soul to put hope in God: "Hope thou in God." Dickson asserts, "The only means of remedying discouragements and unquietness of mind" is to set faith on work to go to God and take hold of Him, and to cast anchor within the vail, hoping for and expecting relief from Him: *hope thou in God.*"[38]

3. Talk yourself out of accepting the lies and devastating innuendos of Satan by mediation upon the truth of God's Word. Discipline the mind to bring "every thought into captivity to the obedience of Christ" (2 Corinthians 10:5 ASV).

4. Promise yourself, as David, deliverance from trouble into a new experience of comfort, consolation, and joy will come from the Lord.[39] "Why are you down in the dumps, dear soul? Why are you crying the blues? Fix my eyes on God—soon I'll be praising again. He puts a smile on my face. He's my God" (Psalm 42:11 MSG). Spurgeon said, "Play the man [like David], and thy castings down shall turn to liftings up, and thy disquietudes to calm."[40]

"There can be no faith so feeble that Christ does not respond."—Alexander Maclaren.

13

David asked: "What is man?"

"What is man, that thou art mindful of him? And the son of man, that thou visitest him?" (Psalm 8:4–6). David questions the reason for God's concern, compassion, and care for man, who is but a "worm." Craige asserts these questions are so asked as to evoke the resounding answer, "Nothing!" He explains, "In such vastness, it is inconceivable that human beings have significance or meaning; it is inconceivable that God could remember each human being or give attention to each person."[41] Yet He does.

Matthew Henry remarks, "Though man is a worm, yet God puts a respect upon him, and shows him an abundance of kindness; man is, above all the creatures in this lower world, the favorite and darling of Providence."[42] Gill states that "God reckons [man] as His portion and inheritance, His jewels and peculiar treasure, and who are as dear to Him as the apple of His eye; whom He 'magnifies,' as in Job 7:17; makes them kings and priests; raises them from the dunghill, and sets them among princes, to inherit the throne of glory; on whom He sets His heart, and loves them with an everlasting love."[43]

Barnes comments, "It is amazing that a being so insignificant as man should be an object of interest to God, or that One so great should pay any attention to him and his affairs."[44] Why does God show interest in people who are diseased with sin from the crown of the head to the sole of the foot? Spurgeon says, "Infinite condescension can alone account for the Lord stooping to be the friend of man. That he should make man the subject of election, the object of redemption, the child of eternal love, the darling of infallible providence, the next of kin to Deity, is indeed a matter requiring more than the two notes of exclamation found in this verse (Psalm 144:3)."[45]

Why is God mindful of sinful man?

1. He is aware of man because He created him in His image. Harman states, "Man occupies a special position in creation, in that he alone of all the creatures was made in the image and likeness of God (Genesis 1:26–27; 5:1)."[46]

2. He is mindful of man because He placed all things under his dominion. James Hasting asserts, "At the summit of creation, God stamped man with the Divine image, crowned him, and gave him

dominion over all creatures. This is the Bible doctrine of the origin of man, and it takes us to the heights."[47]

3. He is mindful of man because of His desire to save him from ruination and damnation (2 Peter 3:9).

4. He is aware of man because it is His nature to show love, compassion, and mercy to broken and bruised people.

5. He is mindful of man because He wants to bring him to repentance (Romans 2:4).

6. He is mindful of man, for He longs for those He created to reign with Him in eternity.

Psalm 8:3–6 stands out in the whole book of Psalms, for it underscores God's love and concern for man despite his contemptible attitude toward God and sin. Man deserves His judgment, not lovingkindness, mercy, and grace. "But God…" (Romans 5:8). Joseph Hall expresses man's response to God's goodness: "How should we be consecrated to Thee above all others since Thou hast bestowed more cost on us than others!"[48]

"Though man is a worm, and the son of man is a worm (Job 25:6), yet God puts respect upon him and shows him an abundance of kindness; man is, above all the creatures in this lower world, the favorite and darling of Providence."[49] —Matthew Henry.

14

Elihu asked: "Where is God my Maker?"

"But none saith, where is God my Maker, who giveth songs in the night; who teacheth us more than the beasts of the earth, and maketh us wiser than the fowls of heaven?" (Job 35:10–11). Elihu's interrogation of Job continues with an accusation of man's disinterest in finding God.

Why do so few inquire after God, their Maker?

1. Absence of spiritual perception. Paul says, "The person without the Spirit does not accept the things that come from the

Spirit of God but considers them foolishness, and cannot understand them because they are discerned only through the Spirit" (1 Corinthians 2:14 NIV). Spurgeon said, "Until divine grace comes in and changes our nature, there is none that saith, 'Where is God my Maker, who giveth songs in the night?'"[50]

2. Spiritual blindness. Satan blinds them from seeing the truth of their need for God (2 Corinthians 4:4). Men are like the lost silver in the parable of the lost coin. Does the silver know that it is lost? Neither do most souls (Luke 15:8–10). Spurgeon said, "If a man wills to see the truth and submits himself to the enlightenment of the Holy Ghost, he will not be left in darkness."[51] The preaching or presentation of the Gospel is the one thing that can open blind eyes to the truth of the gospel (2 Corinthians 3:3–4). Calvin asserts, "The blindness of unbelievers in no way detracts from the clarity of the Gospel; the sun is no less bright because blind men do not perceive its light."

3. Captivity to Satan. "They were captured by him [Satan] to do his will" (2 Timothy 2:26 EHV).

4. Pride. "The wicked in his proud countenance does not seek God; God is in none of his thoughts" (Psalm 10:4 NKJV). C. S. Lewis said, "As long as you are proud, you cannot know God."[52]

5. Love of the world and its pleasures. "Lovers of pleasures more than lovers of God" (2 Timothy 3:4). "They have no taste but for play and amusement, one scene of diversion after another; the hours which should be spent in intercourse with Heaven are prostituted to folly, vanity, and idleness."[53]

6. Hostility toward God. "The mind governed by the flesh is hostile to God" (Romans 8:7 NIV).

7. Stubborn unwillingness to meet God on His terms. The Lord said, "If any man will come after me, let him deny himself, and take up his cross daily, and follow me" (Luke 9:23). Many walk away from God, saying, "This is tough teaching, too tough to swallow" (John 6:60 MSG). Someone said, "If the truth makes you uncomfortable, don't blame the truth....blame the lie that made you comfortable."

8. Too high a cost. Often, man does not inquire after God because the impact it would have on their social life, companionship, or political status is too high a price to pay.

Inquire after God now. "Seek the LORD while He may be found" (Isaiah 55:6 ESV). "Blessed is the man that trusteth in the LORD, and whose hope the LORD is" (Jeremiah 17:7). C. S. Lewis writes, "Faith in Christ is the only thing to save you from despair." T. Kennion asserts, "The great subject for wonder is that while God has revealed Himself as the refuge of the oppressed, a friend in the day of calamity, a Savior from guilt and sin and hell, a comforter in darkness, and a deliverer in trouble, He should be neglected in circumstances and times when no other being and no other object can cheer the heart or interpose any effectual relief."[54] Until that question is seriously asked, peace and meaning in life will be elusive.

"Where is God, my Maker?" The answer is somewhere and everywhere. He is within the seeker's eyesight and reach (Hebrews 11:6). He awaits to be your helper, instructor, comforter, and giver of songs in the night.

"The great subject for wonder is that while God has revealed Himself as the refuge of the oppressed, a friend in the day of calamity, a Savior from guilt and sin and hell, a comforter in darkness, and a deliverer in trouble, He should be neglected in circumstances and times when no other being and no other object can cheer the heart or interpose any effectual relief."—T. Kennion.

15

Elihu asked: "Where is God my Maker, who giveth songs in the night?"

"Where is God my Maker, who giveth songs in the night?" Why does God give songs in the night?

1. God gives saints songs in the night to cheer, comfort, encourage, and instill courage and hope.

2. He gives suffering saints songs in the night to comfort those who bear similar affliction.

3. He gives songs in the night as a testimonial to the world of His faithfulness to His children in adversity.

4. He gives sweet songs in the night to uproot and expel the sour ones.

Note several characteristics of these 'songs in the night.'

1. The source of the song. It's not the saint that creates the song, but "God my maker" (Job 35:10). Hastings wrote, "When, then, our text speaks of God 'who giveth songs in the night,' it means that it belongs to Him to put songs of praise and joy into the Christian's heart in seasons of sorrow and trial. It belongs to God, and to God alone, to give such songs."[55] Spurgeon comments, "Let but this voice be clear and this body full of health, and I can sing God's praise; silence my tongue, lay me upon the bed of languishing, and how shall I then chant God's high praises, unless He Himself give me the song? No, it is not in man's power to sing when all is adverse unless an altar coal shall touch his lip. It was a divine song that Habakkuk sang when in the night (Habakkuk 3:17–18). Then, since our Maker gives songs in the night, let us wait upon Him for the music."[56]

2. The theme of the song. It is composed of various themes, including the richness of God's grace, mercy, and compassion; personal redemption through the blood of Christ; eternal life beyond this land of tears and sorrows; the ever abiding presence of God amid trouble; the second coming of the Lord; the Lord's omnipotence in all and over all; and reunion with the saints in Heaven. Often, God uses the believer's contemplation of His unbreakable promises to birth the songs. Spurgeon said, often, in the dark times, he would find great delight and cheer in songs about the second coming.[57]

3. The recipient of the song. To whom are songs provided at night? Not unto all, but unto redeemed souls. Among the many who bear witness to the soothing and comforting songs that God provides in the night are Paul and Silas in the Philippian jail (Acts 16:34), David in exile (2 Samuel 15:30), Hezekiah on his deathbed (Isaiah

38:20), Paul in imprisonment (Philippians 3:1), and Job in his suffering (Job 19:25–27).

4. The time of the song. David said, "Yet the LORD will command his lovingkindness in the day time, and in the night his song shall be with me" (Psalm 42:8). Night songs are generated in the soul in times of grave calamity, adversity, sickness, sorrow, and suffering to make them bearable and to keep the soul in tune with the source of all comfort and hope as long as the trouble lasts.

5. The medicine of the song. It is the sweet song of Heaven laced with hope, comfort, and peace that soothes the troubled heart by thwarting the terror, fear, despair, and anxiety of the affliction or adversity. Matthew Henry remarks, "He gives songs in the night, that is, when our condition is ever so dark, and sad, and melancholy, there is that in God, in His providence and promise, which is sufficient, not only to support us, but to fill us with joy and consolation, and enable us in everything to give thanks, and even to rejoice in tribulation."[58]

6. The scope of the song. Though the saint is promised a song in the night, a song orchestrated by God, it may not dispel the darkness of the night.[59] The song drives the "darkness" from the heart, not necessarily from the body. God doesn't promise to eradicate our "dark times" but to make them endurable and less disturbing by providing a song in the night.

"It is true under the Gospel that in the day of darkness and calamity, God puts into the mouth the language of praise and fills the heart with thanksgiving."[60]—Albert Barnes.

16

The Israelites asked: "Can God furnish a table in the wilderness?"

"They said, Can God furnish a table in the wilderness?" (Psalm 78:19). Amidst hardships, the Israelites in the wilderness murmured, asking a foolish question: "Can God?" Ludicrous, I say, because God had already proven that He could during the Exodus by delivering them from the plagues, Pharaoh and his army, the mighty waters of the Red Sea, thirst (water from the rock and pure water at Marah), hunger (manna and quail), and led them by the cloud by day and pillar of fire by night (Psalm 78:12–16).

Yet despite these miraculous deeds, unbelief in God's ability to provide "a table in the wilderness" (Psalm 78:19) was expressed. They "unbelievingly and defiantly demanded, instead of trustfully waiting and praying" (Delitzsch). The saint that trusts God need not question the ability and readiness of God to intervene in times of trouble or sorrow. Spurgeon states, "To question the ability of one who is manifestly Almighty is to speak against Him." Says Matthew Henry, "Those that set bounds to God's power speak against Him." To the question, "Can God?" the saint readily responds, "Yes, God can!"

The curious servants of Hezekiah perhaps asked about the possibility of his recovery, "Can God?" Before Isaiah was hardly out the door, it was thundered, "God can" (2 Kings 20:1–5).

When the three Hebrew children were cast into the fiery furnace, Nebuchadnezzar and soldiers alike asked, "Can God?" When they witnessed the fourth man in the fire and all walking around unharmed, they answered, "God can" (Daniel 3:25). When Daniel was put into a den of lions, Darius asked, "Can God?" Early the following day, he learned, "God can." When the widow of Zarephath and her son were famished with hunger, she asked, "Can God?" Long afterward, the miraculous jar of oil and flour still provided the need. She discovered "God can" (1 Kings 17:7–16).

Our God is a God that can!

"They who will not be content will speak against providence even when it daily loadeth them with benefits."[61] —C. H. Spurgeon.

17

The Israelites asked: "How shall we sing the Lord's song in a strange land?"

"By the rivers of Babylon, there we sat down, yea, we wept, when we remembered Zion. We hanged our harps upon the willows in the midst thereof. For there they that carried us away captive required of us a song; and they that wasted us required of us mirth, saying, Sing us one of the songs of Zion. How shall we sing the Lord's song in a strange land?" (Psalm 137:1–4).

The "Lord's song" includes the Psalms, hymns, and spiritual songs, all of which are the making of melody in the heart to the Lord (Ephesians 5:19). The "Lord's song" may be "sung" verbally or mentally. This song was silenced among the saints in Babylonian captivity due to the heaviness of heart (grief and sorrow over their estate and that of Jerusalem). Without a song to sing (in a "strange land," a solemn place where the believer's song is silenced by tribulation and trials), he hangs his "harp" upon the willows at the river's bank (for he has no heart to use it) and tearfully inquires, "How shall we sing the Lord's song in a strange land?" Spurgeon says, "Sad indeed is the child of sorrow when he grows weary of his harp [and song], from which in better days he had been able to draw sweet solaces."[62]

> Our harps, which used their part to bear,
> When Zion's songs we sung,
> On willow trees that flourished there,
> As useless now, we hung.
> —John Barnard (1681–1770)

"How shall we sing the Lord's song in a strange land?" What a good question! While languishing in "a strange land" (sickness, suffering, sorrow, or approaching death), how is the saint to sing the song of Zion? How is it that martyrs of old, while dying for the faith, still had a song as they were nailed to a cross, thrust into a den of lions, beheaded by the guillotine, or burned at the stake? How is it that saints like Fanny Crosby, blinded in infancy by a medical mistake; Joni Eareckson Tada, who through a swimming accident became quadriplegic; Horatio Spafford, whose children were drowned at sea when crossing the Atlantic, all maintained their song despite the pain, suffering, sickness, and sorrow? Along with multitudes of others, in their "strange land," these testify with Job, "Though he slay me, yet will I trust in him" (Job 13:15). Nothing was able to silence their song. G. Campbell Morgan says, "Any man can sing when the prison doors are open, and he is set free. The Christian soul sings in prison."

Suffering saints like these answer the question, "How shall we sing the Lord's song in a strange land?" with the question, why shouldn't we sing the Lord's song in a strange land? They say, "God is the same God in this land as He is outside it; not one iota has changed about His loving guardianship and tender compassionate care. Every promise of the Bible remains true—possession of forgiveness of sin and eternal life through the Savior's redeeming blood has not been altered; the defiled garments of sin are still washed clean; the saints' citizenship in Heaven is unchanged; God yet remains in sovereign control of all that happens to the saint; the Holy Spirit's ministry of comfort and help to the believer is unabated; and God's mercies are still new every morning."

These stupendous facts ought to cause the heart to erupt in praise songs to the King, even while sojourning in a "strange land," and to say with David, "I will bless the LORD at all times: his praise shall continually be in my mouth" (Psalm 34:1).

"The Lord's song will sound forever in Heaven, but shall we be there to sing it?"[63]—Dean Vaughan.

18

Solomon asked: "Who hath woe? Who hath sorrow?"

"Who hath woe? Who hath sorrow? Who hath contentions? Who hath babbling? Who hath wounds without cause? Who hath redness of eyes? They that tarry long at the wine; they that go to seek mixed wine" (Proverbs 23:29–30). Maclaren asserts, "The questions, six in number, fall into three pairs, which deal respectively with the man's feelings of discomfort, his relations with others, and his physical sufferings."[64]

Solomon states the danger and harm of alcohol consumption (Proverbs 23:32–35).

1. Alcohol is like the fangs of a rattlesnake full of venomous poison awaiting an unexpected passer-by (Proverbs 23:32). Once alcohol is consumed, its poison is released into the body to do its deadly, destructive work. It kills the brain cells, deadens the senses, retards the reflexes, damages glands and vital organs, and initiates the process of death.

2. Alcohol is like a robber who steals all one possesses, leaving him in deep poverty. "For the drunkard and the glutton shall come to poverty: and drowsiness shall clothe a man with rags" (Proverbs 23:21).

3. Alcohol is like Mr. Hyde taking over Dr. Jekyll's speech, leading him to say unruly and embarrassing things. "Thine heart shall utter perverse things" (Proverbs 23:33b).

4. Alcohol is like a man in the ocean under its control being tossed to and fro, unaware of what's happening. "Yea, thou shalt be as he that lieth down in the midst of the sea" (Proverbs 23:34).

5. Alcohol is like a mule whose blinders are removed, and his eyes are free to roam the terrain (the forbidden), resulting in impure conduct. Alcohol retards mental rationality and deteriorates walls of sexual restraint. "Thine eyes shall behold strange women" (Proverbs 23:33).

6. Alcohol is like a man getting beat up in a fight, unaware of the harm received; he denies the hurt that alcohol produces in his life. "And you will say, 'They hit me, but I didn't feel it. I didn't even know it when they beat me up'" (Proverbs 23:35 NLT).

7. Alcohol is like the tyrant that enslaves a person to serve him alone; the drunkard can't wait until he sleeps off his intoxication so he can drink again. "When will I wake up so I can look for another drink?" (Proverbs 23:35b NLT).

8. Alcohol is like a pretender, pretending to give a person gusto in life only to give sorrow. "Wine is a mocker, strong drink is raging: and whosoever is deceived thereby is not wise" (Proverbs 20:1).

9. Alcohol is the mother of sorrows and the father of trouble. "Who has anguish? Who has sorrow? Who is always fighting? Who

is always complaining? Who has unnecessary bruises? Who has bloodshot eyes? It is the one who spends long hours in the taverns, trying out new drinks" (Proverbs 23:29–30 NLT).

H. A. Ironside says, "Wine has its place. Scripture recognizes its medicinal virtue, and a lawful use of it also when needed (1 Timothy 5:23). But how easily it becomes a snare that destroys the will and wrecks the life."[65] Note, alcohol's place in the early church was for medicinal use, not recreational.

"The most dangerous drug in America is beverage alcohol."[66]—Adrian Rogers.

19

Nehemiah asked: "Why should the work cease?"

"I am doing a great work, so that I cannot come down: why should the work cease, whilst I leave it, and come down to you?" (Nehemiah 6:3). Nehemiah, in rebuilding the walls of Jerusalem and restoring worship within the Temple, encountered fierce opposition from Sanballat and Tobiah which was withstood courageously and successfully. In just fifty-two days, the work was accomplished (Nehemiah 6:15).

Note ten factors that contributed to Nehemiah's success in the task.

1. The work was not chosen by Nehemiah but assigned by God (Nehemiah 2:12). Spurgeon says, "If you are not certain that the work you are about was given to you of God…you have no business to enter upon the work at all, for your whole strength will lie in a full conviction that your Master has sent you."

2. The work was undertaken with the right attitude (Nehemiah 6:3). To every effort of the enemy to deter Nehemiah from the work, he said, "I'm doing a great work."

3. The work was counted as a priority (Nehemiah 6:3–4). His fundamental principle in the work was never to leave the building for the battling.

4. The work was urgently undertaken (Nehemiah 6:3). The clock is ticking on the time available to accomplish an assigned task. We tend to forget that. Nehemiah didn't.

5. The work was undergirded with prayer from the start to completion (Nehemiah 6:9). Redpath states, "In Christian work, organizing and agonizing should go together."

6. The work was graphed by a vision of what needed to be done and how (Nehemiah 2:13–15). Note, God's minister, in surveying the rubbish and broken-down walls of the church, is to be inflamed with a vision inflamed by the Holy Spirit for undertaking its restoration.

7. The work was sustained through perseverance (Nehemiah 6:3). Nehemiah and the people endured slander (Nehemiah 6:6–7), ridicule (Nehemiah 4:3), and physical assault (Nehemiah 4:7–8) through God's enabling strength (Nehemiah 6:9). Note, "Men in high places are little to be envied. They are often exposed to special dangers, both in principle and person."

8. The work was shouldered by most of the people (Nehemiah 2:18). Nehemiah didn't believe in a one-person ministry. Success in the minister's work hinges on the participation of church members. Spurgeon said, "Union is strength."

9. The work was preserved through Nehemiah's discernment (Nehemiah 6:12–13). Nehemiah discerned Shemaiah's plot to mar his reputation and discredit his leadership before the people. To safeguard reputation, work, and ministry, the minister must "test the spirits" to see if they are of God.

10. The work was orchestrated and "wrought" by God from start to finish (Nehemiah 6:16). Nehemiah didn't have a *How to Build a Wall* handbook. But he did have God's divine authorization, supervision, and empowerment for the work. Redpath states, "Nehemiah triumphed because he was doing a work which God initiated; and because God initiated it, God Himself empowered it. It never would have succeeded had God not begun it."

"Hard work will do almost everything, but in God's service, it must not only be hard work, but hot work. The heart must be on fire."—C. H. Spurgeon.

20

Paul asked: "For if the trumpet give an uncertain sound, who shall prepare himself to the battle?"

"For if the trumpet gives an uncertain sound, who shall prepare himself to the battle?" (1 Corinthians 14:8 JUB). In biblical times, the trumpet was used to assemble the army, warn of impending danger to a city, commemorate the year of Jubilee, crown the king, warn of the enemy's attack, and, in battle, order an attack and stop it. Different sounds (toots or notes) were played for each occasion so there would be no mix-up as to what was meant. Can you imagine the mass confusion when the trumpeter of the city played the wrong sound (like signaling the king's crowning when he should have sounded the note for an invading army)?

Apply the principle to the act of preaching. "For if the trumpet [the preaching of the preacher] gives an uncertain sound, who shall prepare himself to the battle?" Some of the failures of modern-day preaching to win the lost are traceable to its "hearers," but often, it is due to the "uncertain sound" trumpeted by the preacher.

1. An uncertain sound from the preacher is an unprepared sound. Saith Spurgeon, "Habitually to come into the pulpit unprepared is unpardonable presumption; nothing can more effectually lower ourselves and our office."

2. An uncertain sound from the preacher is an unanointed sound. Martyn Lloyd-Jones has succinctly asserted, "If there is no power, there is no preaching." Paul preached "in demonstration of the Spirit and of power" (1 Corinthians 2:4). Ellicott comments, "The Apostle's demonstration of the truth of the Gospel was the result of no human art or skill, but came from the Spirit and power of God, and therefore the Corinthians could glory in no human teacher, but only in the power of God, which was the true source of the success of the Gospel amongst them."

3. An uncertain sound from the preacher is an unscriptural sound. Roy Fish stated, "Much preaching has become the theories of men rather than the Word of God. Sermons have become psychological doses of uplift." Saith Spurgeon, "The Spirit of God

bears no witness to Christless sermons. Leave Jesus out of your preaching, and the Holy Spirit will never come upon you." Hold fast to and proclaim "sound words [doctrine]" (2 Timothy 1:13).

4. An uncertain sound from the preacher is an incomplete sound. With Paul, the man of God must 'not shun to declare all the counsel of God' (Acts 20:27). He must tell the whole of the Gospel story without alteration.

5. An uncertain sound from the preacher is an unclear sound. The preacher must jettison the language of Zion and use words that connect with the person in the pew. A minister ended his sermon: "And now, my friends, if you do not believe these truths, there may be grave eschatological consequences for you."

Afterward, a layman asked the preacher, "Did you mean that they would be in danger of Hell?"

"Why, yes," he replied.

"Then why in the world didn't you say so?" the layman inquired. Matthew Henry remarked, "Words without a meaning can convey no notion nor instruction to the mind, and words not understood have no meaning with those who do not understand them; to talk to them in such language is to waste our breath."[67]

6. An uncertain sound from the preacher is an ineffectual sound. Preaching void of the power of the Holy Spirit and absent of plain scriptural exposition may be eloquent, flowery, and appealing but will avail nothing.

"The trumpets which blew down the walls of Jericho were trumpets which gave no uncertain sound."[68]—J. C. Ryle.

21

Eliphaz asked: "Are the consolations of God small with thee?"

"Are the consolations of God small with thee?" (Job 15:11). Eliphaz questions Job whether or not the hopes he and his friends shared about God were sufficient to humble him and prompt his repentance.

"Are the consolations of God small with thee?" Is the comfort God supplies amid bodily suffering, incurable illness, grievous sorrow, and excruciating trouble enough? When does it seem the consolations, the comfort of God of every kind and in every degree, are too small?

1. When they are slow in coming. Impatience with affliction, infirmity, and disappointment over a slow resolution prompt a person to count God's consolations as insufficient.

2. When they fail to do what is wanted. The prayer for deliverance must be concluded with what our Lord prayed in the garden when facing death, 'Not my will, but thy will be done.'

3. When the person is ready to give up battling the affliction.

4. When they are left untried. The consolations of God must be utilized in faith to be efficacious. David says, "Taste and see that the Lord is good. Oh, the joys of those who take refuge in him!" (Psalm 34:8 NLT). And James says, "Ye have not, because ye ask not" (James 4:2).

5. When they are devalued and lightly esteemed. "These consolations are not small in themselves and, therefore, ought not to be lightly esteemed by us. They lay a foundation for peace and comfort under the greatest afflictions."[69]

6. When they are heartily denied. The consolations of the Lord must be freely received in the spirit of faith. Brooks says, "All that there is consolatory in God—being, sympathy, truth, power—Christ has set in the clearness and the splendor of His life. If you want consolation, you must come to Him."[70]

7. When the person lives in neglect of the Holy Spirit, who is the comforter.

"Are the consolations of God small with thee?" Multitudes, from experience, testify they are not. If they are small with thee, based upon what has been shared, is it not your own fault?

"The consolations of God not being small in themselves, it is very lamentable if they are small with us. It is a great affront to God and evidence of a degenerate depraved mind to disesteem and undervalue spiritual delights."—Matthew Henry.

22

A Lawyer asked: "Who is my neighbor?"

"Who is my neighbor?" (Luke 10:29). Jesus states in the parable of the Good Samaritan (Luke 10:30–37) that a neighbor is anyone in *legitimate* need. Timothy Keller said, "By depicting a Samaritan helping a Jew, Jesus could not have found a more forceful way to say that anyone at all in need—regardless of race, politics, class, and religion—is your neighbor. Not everyone is your brother or sister in faith, but everyone is your neighbor, and you must love your neighbor."

The Samaritan in the narrative is an exemplary example of a neighbor in the way he helped a dying man on the road to Jericho.

1. He helped him without questions. There was no interrogation to determine whether he would help the injured man. He just did.

2. He helped him without thought of cost. "The compassion of this Samaritan was not an idle compassion."[71] The Samaritan bandaged the man's wounds and paid for his stay and care at an inn in full (Luke 10:34–35).

3. He helped him without fear. In a culture where the Jews despised the Samaritans, and the Samaritans the Jews, the man courageously crossed the race barrier to help a neighbor in need.

The parable points out that our neighbors are everyone, not just people who share our ethnicity, nationality, faith, and political views. Martin Luther King, Sr., said, "The first question which the priest and the Levite asked was, 'If I stop to help this man, what will happen to me?' But the Good Samaritan reversed the question: 'If I do not stop to help this man, what will happen to him?'"

4. He helped him without regard to religion or belief. Despite the man being of different faith and race, the Samaritan befriended him.

5. He helped him without the thought of being inconvenienced. Unlike the priest and Levite, the injured man's need for help outweighed the Good Samaritan's schedule. Note, the Samaritan went the second mile in showing kindness to the man by staying at an inn with him to ensure his care.

6. He helped him without compensation. The Samaritan didn't help the man contingent on the man returning the good done.

7. He helped him without debate or delay.

8. He helped him without passing the buck to another. The man didn't leave the man on the road for another to help, like the priest and Levite had. He took responsibility for him.

As good a model as the Samaritan is of a neighbor, we have a higher model. Spurgeon says, "What the Samaritan gave to the poor man was generous, but it is not comparable to what the Lord Jesus has given to us. He gave him wine and oil, but Jesus has given His heart's-blood to heal our wounds; he lent himself with all his care and thoughtfulness, but Christ gave Himself even to the death for us."[72]

"It is sad when those who should be examples of charity are prodigies of cruelty, and when those who should, by displaying the mercies of God, open the bowels of compassion in others, shut up their own."[73]—Matthew Henry.

23

The Rich Young Ruler asked: "What shall I do that I may inherit eternal life?"

"What shall I do that I may inherit eternal life?" (Mark 10:17c). Note the rich young ruler's quest for salvation.

1. He came to the right person: Jesus (Mark 10:17a). He sought Jesus out not only because He is the door to salvation but also because He loves the down and out, the broken and weary, the sinful and guilty. "Jesus beholding him loved him" (Mark 10:21). No one loves a man or desires his best good and end as Jesus does (John 3:16).

2. He came with the right attitude: kneeling (Mark 10:17b). Saith Matthew Henry, "He kneeled to Him in token of the great value and veneration he had for Him as a Teacher come from God, and his earnest desire to be taught by Him. He bowed the knee to the Lord Jesus as one that would not only *do obeisance* to him now but would *yield obedience* to him always; he bowed the knee as one that meant *to bow the soul to him.*"

3. He came with the right question: "What shall I do that I may inherit eternal life?" (Mark 10:17c). The man believed in life after death and that something had to be done to be entitled to it. Thus, he asks earnestly, "What shall I do that I may inherit eternal life?" Man's most important question is how to be made right with Holy God and gain Heaven at death.

4. He got the right answer: "Come, take up the cross, and follow me" (Mark 10:21). Following Christ requires repentance, faith, and an unrivaled love for Him.

5. He made the wrong decision: "He...went away grieved" (Mark 10:22). He chose to cling to the world and its possessions. Steeped in legalism, the youth thought keeping the commandments and good deeds would gain him eternal life. When told that such was not the case, that it required the placing of one's entire life upon the altar in surrender to Christ as Lord and Savior, he was sorrowful, "for he had great possessions" (Mark 10:22b). The desire to gain eternal life was overtaken by the want of the stuff of the world. 'And you would not come to me that you might have life.' Courson asserts, "This is the only instance in the Bible where a man comes and kneels before Jesus and leaves worse off than when he came."[74]

"Sinners are not ready for the good news of the Gospel until they accept the bad news that the law condemns them as guilty sinners."[75]—John MacArthur.

24

Belshazzar asked: "Are you the Daniel brought from Israel as a captive by King Nebuchadnezzar?"

"The king asked him, "Are you the Daniel brought from Israel as a captive by King Nebuchadnezzar?" (Daniel 5:13 TLB). Daniel served the Lord for over 70 years and was in his eighties when Belshazzar summoned him out of retirement to interpret the meaning of the mysterious handwriting on the wall (Daniel 5:13–14). Daniel hastily responded.

1. Retired ministers are often forgotten and overlooked despite their rich experience, vast knowledge, and godliness. Matthew Henry observes, "There are a great many valuable men, and such as might be made very useful, that lie long buried in obscurity, and some that have done eminent services that live to be overlooked and taken no notice of. But whatever men are, God is not unrighteous to forget the services done to His kingdom. Being turned out of his place, Daniel lived privately and sought no opportunity to come into notice again, yet he lived near the court and within call."

2. A time will come when a Belshazzar will summon the retired Daniel for help. As a retired Daniel, live in expectation and readiness for that day. You might be ignored and snubbed now. Just bide your time. The hour will come when coldness or conflict in the church, a crisis in a person's life, or chaos in the world will prompt a summons for your expertise, knowledge, and wisdom. Belshazzar will turn to the man in touch with God when a pressing need arises or when reminded of him by another who knows of his life and work (Daniel 5:15–16).

3. The retired minister must stay ready for the summons to serve. "Live near the court and within call," prepared to assist when asked.

4. When utilized, retired ministers provide invaluable benefits. Daniel interpreted the King's dream and played an important role in the nation's government. "They clothed Daniel with scarlet, and put a chain of gold about his neck, and made a proclamation concerning him, that he should be the third ruler in the kingdom" (Daniel 5:29).

Despite years of distinguished and faithful ministry, a retired Daniel lives in large part in comparative obscurity near your church. They live "near the court and within call" but are often ignored and overlooked. What a tragedy. What a waste. What a shame. And the church and kingdom of God are the poorer for it. Let him that possesses the influence and platform to encourage churches, colleges, camps, and schools use the theological knowledge (Daniel 5:11–12), spiritual wisdom (Daniel 5:11), and practical experience (Daniel 5:12) of a retired Daniel!

"You will be wanted someday by Belshazzar."—Joseph Parker.

25

Elisha asked: "Where fell it?"

"Where fell it?" (2 Kings 6:6). Due to the lack of room for ministerial students at Elisha's college, an effort was undertaken to build another dormitory, which required the borrowing of at least one axe (2 Kings 6:5–7). And it was lost in the water as a tree was being hewn to the ground. The axe head symbolizes the power of the Holy Spirit in Christian work, which may be lost.

"Where fell it?"

1. The axe head surfaced at the exact spot in the water where it was lost. When power is lost, go back to the place where it departed.

2. Without an axe head, the work is futile. The work of God demands Holy Ghost empowerment. It's foolish to attempt to cut down trees (do God's work in preaching, singing, teaching, witnessing) with only an axe handle (abilities of the flesh). Yet, that's what some attempt to do, and they wonder why there is little or no success.

3. Working without knowing the axe head is lost is possible. "Strangers have devoured his strength, and he knoweth it not: yea, gray hairs are here and there upon him, yet he knoweth not" (Hosea 7:9). It is disheartening to see a person absent of power minister as though he had power. Recall Samson (Judges 16:20). Guard against becoming a dry shadow of what you used to be, a man mighty in power.

4. The lost axe head may be recovered. As Elisha instructed, "the man reached out and grabbed it" from the water (2 Kings 6:7 NLT). Christ bids all that have lost their axe head (power) to reach out to Him in faith to have it (the fullness of the Holy Spirit) restored (Luke 11:11–13). Note, God used Elisha to help the distraught student reclaim the source of his power for the work. "The iron did swim." For whom might God enable you to do the same?

5. There was no future work for the young Bible college student until the axe head was found. And there's no future for us until we discover where we lost our power and recover it.

"Contrary to all expectation, the iron was made to mount from the depth of the stream and to swim; for things impossible with man are possible with God."[76]—C. H. Spurgeon.

26

David asked: "If the foundations be destroyed, what can the righteous do?"

"If the foundations be destroyed, what can the righteous do?" (Psalm 11:3). The "foundations" are the pillars upon which the fundamental principles of law and justice rest in society set in place by Sovereign God at creation and maintained. "The righteous" refers to those who are upright and godly. The question posed is one that has been asked by the righteous time and again in the face of sweeping anti-Christian legislation and cultural reform. It is being asked more and more as "political correctness" and "cancel culture" replace biblical and moral values, and Christians are being persecuted and ostracized.

What can the righteous do? They must not be dissuaded from insistence on allegiance to Almighty God and His holy decrees in Scripture. They must not succumb to the evil tide but resist it with every tooth and nail. They must not cowardly flee the struggle. Like David, they must refuse to "flee to the mountains" but be vigilant in the battle for the right, depending upon the power and authority of God for ultimate victory. "In the Lord put I my trust."

Spurgeon asserts, "David here declares the great source of his unflinching courage. He borrows his light from Heaven—from the great central orb of Deity....'What can the righteous do in an unrighteous government?'" To the question, Spurgeon answers, "'What can they not do?' when they trust in God, who reigns supreme in authority and power, praying for His divine intervention and protection (Psalm 11:4–7)." J. M. Boice said, "What can the righteous do? They can go on being righteous. And they can stand against the evil of their society." The righteous must persevere courageously, saying with Edward Mote, "When all around my soul gives way, He then is all my hope and stay."

What can the righteous do when the foundations are destroyed? We must keep looking to God, who sits on the throne in steadfast hope, and trust (Psalm 11:4–6). "This vision of God's eternal reality lifts us above every earthly threat."[77]

"When the foundations are taken out from under us, the righteous have God to cling to."[78]—J. Vernon McGee.

27

Solomon asked: "A wounded spirit who can bear?"

"The spirit of a man will sustain his infirmity; but a wounded spirit who can bear?" (Proverbs 18:14). A wounded spirit (broken, damaged, or crushed spirit) is the painful injury to the heart (emotions). Lawson says, "A wounded spirit is intolerable. It is a very hell upon earth and has often made the most courageous of men, and the best of saints, to roar through the disquiet of their hearts."[79]

The wounded spirit results from abuse, betrayal, sorrow, desertion, slander, scorn, belittlement, hypercriticism, and insult. Left unchecked, it precipitates pain, hurt, resentment, retaliation, hostility, feelings of inferiority, and inner turmoil. An unrelenting focus on the injury and unforgiveness toward the offender fuels it. Its cure or healing is found in three things.

1. Forgiveness of the offender. Arterburn said, "When we hold fast to resentment, we chain ourselves to a pain we cannot undo. The alternative is to move on, give up our right to resent, and find a way to forgive." Mark Twain said, "Forgiveness is the fragrance that the violet sheds on the heel that has crushed it." Forgiveness is not based on an offender's desert, but on our Lord's example (Colossians 3:13) and instruction (Ephesians 4:32).

2. Couple forgiveness with a pledge not to mention the offense again. The promise, per Jay Adams, is threefold: "You promise not to remember his sin by bringing it up to him, to others, or to yourself. The sin is buried."[80] And don't allow others to bring it up. When someone wants to dig up a buried wound, refuse to give them a shovel.

3. Abide in Christ; His presence will heal the hurt and pain (Isaiah 61:1). "He healeth the broken in heart, and bindeth up their wounds" (Psalm 147:3). Spurgeon says, "He deigns to handle and heal broken hearts. He himself lays on the ointment of grace, and

the soft bandages of love, and thus binds up the bleeding wounds of those convinced of sin. Come, broken hearts, come to the Physician who never fails to heal; uncover your wounds to him who so tenderly binds them up!"[81]

"God will mend a broken heart if you give Him all the pieces."—Aesop.

28

Paul asked: "Know ye not that those who run in a race all run, but one receiveth the prize?"

"Know ye not that those who run in a race all run, but one receiveth the prize? So run, that ye may obtain it" (1 Corinthians 9:24 KJ21). Paul had accomplished much—thousands of converts and disciples, thirteen Bible books, three missionary journeys that expanded the kingdom. He possessed an extensive and powerful influence among kings and paupers. All this, he realized, would be "loss" through a "rule" infraction if slothful in spiritual discipline.

D. K. Lowery suggests, "Like the brother who had indulged in immorality (1 Corinthians 5:1–5), Paul's life could be cut short by the disciplinary disapproval of God."[82] All this he feared and took steps to prevent it. Thus, Paul said, "So I run with purpose in every step. I am not just shadowboxing. I discipline my body like an athlete, training it to do what it should. Otherwise, I fear that after preaching to others I myself might be *disqualified*" (1 Corinthians 9:26–27 NLT). Saith Donald Grey Barnhouse, "Godly fear made him live like a runner in a race, hurling himself toward the goal with no thought of any other circumstance."[83]

The knowledge that violating the "rules" would result in God's disapproval, disqualification, and loss of reward incited him not to "faint." He writes, "Each one's work will be clearly shown [for what it is]; for the day [of judgment] will disclose it, because it is to be revealed with fire, and the fire will test the quality and character and worth of each person's work. If any person's work which he has built [on this foundation, that is, any outcome of his effort] remains [and survives this test], he will receive a reward. But if any person's work is burned up [by the test], he will suffer the loss [of his reward]; yet he himself will be saved, but only as [one who has barely escaped] through fire" (1 Corinthians 3:13–15 AMP). See 2 Corinthians 5:10.

Maclaren explains, "He shall lose, in that he will stand further from the Lord, and because he can contain less of His glory. His crown is far less resplendent than the others. His seat at Christ's table in the kingdom is far lower. His Heaven is narrower and less radiant. These two are like two vessels, one of which comes into the harbor with a rich freight and flying colors and is welcomed with the tumult of acclaim. The other strikes the bar. 'Some on boards, and some on broken pieces of the ship, all come safe to land.' But ship and cargo, and profit of the venture, are all lost. 'He shall suffer loss, but he himself shall be saved.'"[84]

Stay focused. Guard each step. Don't get disqualified. Don't blemish the good accomplished. Don't become a castaway. Finish well the race that you may attest with Paul, "I have fought a good fight, I have finished my course, I have kept the faith: Henceforth there is laid up for me a crown of righteousness, which the Lord, the righteous judge, shall give me at that day: and not to me only, but unto all them also that love his appearing" (2 Timothy 4:7–8).

"You must keep to the course; you must keep straight on; you must not stop on the road, or turn aside from it, but, urged on by Divine grace, you must ever fly onwards, 'like an arrow from the bow, shot by an archer strong.' And never rest until the march is ended, and you are made pillars in the house of your God."[85]— C. H. Spurgeon.

29

Job asked: "What profit should we have if we pray unto Him?"

"What profit should we have, if we pray unto Him?" (Job 21:15). Job asserts that the wicked, who argue against God and religion, claim no value or benefit in prayer.

But the ungodly are wrong. Prayer is profitable in at least five ways.

1. Prayer enables you to reach further. Prayer transcends time and space to accomplish God's purposes. Duwel comments, "Not only can prayer reach Heaven, but the arm of prayer can span the miles to any part of the world; and you in your place of intercession can touch someone who needs you, even thousands of miles away. This is not make-believe. It is a spiritual reality." T. J. Bach says, "Many of us cannot reach the mission fields on our feet, but we can reach them on our knees."

2. Prayer enables you to go deeper. Talking to God forges one's relationship with Him. The Bible says, "Draw nigh to God, and He will draw nigh to you" (James 4:8). Bounds said, "Prayer makes a godly man, and puts within him the mind of Christ, the mind of humility, of self-surrender, of service, of pity, and of prayer. If we pray, we will become more like God, or else we will quit praying."

3. Prayer enables you to soar higher. "Prayer lifts the soul into the heavens where it hugs God in an indescribable embrace." David said, "I waited patiently for God to help me; then he listened and heard my cry. He lifted me out of the pit of despair, out from the bog and the mire, and set my feet on a hard, firm path, and steadied me as I walked along" (Psalm 40:1–2 TLB).

4. Prayer enables you to succeed greater. Wiersbe says, "Lack of prayer paralyzes us so that we're not able to do anything that will produce lasting fruit to the glory of God."[86] Bounds says, "The man who truly prays gets from God many things denied the prayerless man." James states, "Ye have not, because ye ask not" (James 4:2). Wesley said, "Every new victory which the soul gains is the effect of a new prayer." Graham said, "A prayerless Christian is a powerless Christian."

5. Prayer enables you to see clearer. Pray for better vision and eyesight spiritually. The Bible says, "If you want to know what God wants you to do, ask him, and he will gladly tell you, for he is always ready to give a bountiful supply of wisdom to all who ask him; he

will not resent it" (James 1:5 TLB). The psalmist said, "O Lord, you give me light; you dispel my darkness" (Psalm 18:28 GNT).

"There cannot be an answer until there is a prayer."— Woodrow Kroll.

30

Pilate asked: "What will you do with Jesus?"

"Pilate said unto them, 'What shall I do then with Jesus, who is called Christ?'" (Matthew 27:22 KJ21). To escape the responsibility of Jesus' fate, which was his alone to make, Pilate put it in the hands of the crowd who in unison said, "Let him be crucified."

"What shall I do then with Jesus?" The question suggests other questions whose answers indicate what the answer should be.

1. What can a person do with Jesus? It's not a multiple-choice question with a dozen possible answers but one with only two choices. A person can accept Jesus as Lord and Savior or reject Him. He can follow Him or turn away from Him. He can say yes to Him or no to Him. He does not have the choice of neutrality. Pilate didn't. No man does.

> Jesus is standing in Pilate's hall—
> Friendless, forsaken, betrayed by all.
> Hearken! What meaneth the sudden call!
> What will you do with Jesus?
>
> What will you do with Jesus?
> Neutral, you cannot be.
> – Albert B. Simpson (1905)

2. Who is to decide its answer? Pilate could not shift its answer to others. No man can. Every person must decide it personally. Another's persuasion to answer the question rightly, like Pilate's wife sought him to do, is commendable and mandated by the Lord (Acts 1:8). But ultimately, a man must decide for himself the place

he will give to Christ. "A man convinced against his will is unconvinced still."

3. Why should a person choose for Christ? What is done with Christ is crucial because He, alone, can forgive sin, make man right with God, and give meaning and happiness to life. What is done with Christ is crucial because He, alone, can save man from an eternity in Hell and give him a home in Heaven. What is done with Christ is crucial because He, alone, enables people to maximize their influence for Him over others for time and eternity.

4. When is the right time to decide the question? The Bible answers, "Now is the accepted time; behold, now is the day of salvation" (2 Corinthians 6:2). Delay is not only the thief of time but of the soul.

What will you do with Jesus? Note, at the Judgment, the question will be changed to: What *did* you do with Jesus?

"There are only two kinds of people in the end: those who say to God, 'Thy will be done,' and those to whom God says, in the end, 'Thy will be done.' All that are in Hell choose it."[87]—C. S. Lewis.

31

Amos asked: "Can two walk together, unless they be agreed?"

"Can two walk together, unless they be agreed?" (Amos 3:3). The rhetorical question gives reason for Israel's breached fellowship with God—red-hot rebellion toward Him and mere fleshly religious observances. They were guilty of the same sin as the Pharisees, whom Jesus sternly rebuked, saying, "This people draweth nigh unto me with their mouth, and honoureth me with their lips; but their heart is far from me" (Matthew 15:8). As a result, judgment was pronounced.

What severs the believer's fellowship, walk of unison with God?

1. Disagreement severs fellowship. We cannot walk with God in fellowship unless we agree with Him about His Word, work, and plan.

2. Distance severs fellowship. To walk with God, the soul must abide in Him (John 15:4). J. C. Ryle asserts, "Abide in Me, says Jesus. Cling to Me. Stick fast to Me. Live the life of close and intimate communion with Me. Get nearer to Me. Roll every burden on Me. Cast your whole weight on Me. Never let go of your hold on Me for a moment. Be, as it were, rooted and planted in Me. Do this, and I will never fail you. I will ever abide in you."

3. Darkness severs fellowship. John says, "If we claim, 'We have fellowship with him,' and live in the darkness, we are lying and do not act truthfully" (1 John 1:6 CEB). God has no fellowship with unholy souls. Maclaren says, "At the bottom, there is only one thing that separates a soul from God, and that is a sin of some sort."[88] Light and darkness cannot co-exist. Paul argues, "What communion hath light with darkness?" (2 Corinthians 6:14). Clovis Chappell comments, "Whenever you make up your mind to refuse to go where God wants you to go and to do what God wants you to do, you must make up your mind at the same time to renounce the friendship of God. You cannot walk with Him and at the same time be in rebellion against Him. God has no possible way of entering into fellowship with the soul that is disobedient to His will."[89]

4. Disdain severs fellowship. Enmity separates man from God. "The mind governed by the flesh is hostile to God" (Romans 8:7 NIV).

> Abide in Christ—this highest blessing gain;
> Each day sweet fellowship with Him maintain.
> Abiding, He and we are joined as one;
> In constant fellowship, all barriers gone.
> —Frederick Atkinson (1841–1896)

The highest honor that may be paid to a man at his death is that said of Enoch: "Enoch walked with God."

"To 'walk with God' implies a state of concord and co-operation."[90]—Henry Melvill.

32

Job asked: "Shall vain words [words that fail to comfort] have an end?"

"I have heard many such things: miserable comforters are ye all. Shall vain words have an end?" (Job 16:2–3). In Job's distress, friends did much wrong in their efforts to console him. "They were none at all and worse than none," says Gill, in their attempt to comfort him. Job testifies the friends were 'deceitful brooks' (Job 6:15) and "worthless physicians" (Job 13:4, NIV) but also calls them "miserable comforters" (Job 16:2).

1. What was said was Well-meaning. Job's friends tried to console him. When they heard of the tragedy, they immediately prayed for him and discussed how they might grant him consolation. Their grief was so heavy for Job that they could not speak for seven days. (Their silence proved more beneficial than their debating and arguing.) Credit them for their compassion for Job despite saying unfounded and distressing things.

2. What was said was Wrong. To suggest that the affliction was the consequence of a crime, secret sin, or hypocrisy necessitating immediate repentance for recovery was insensitive and grossly fallacious. There had been no such sin or wicked deed done. "The patient's case is sad indeed when his medicines are poisons and his physicians his worst disease."[91] Note that a person may share biblical truth and teaching with the troubled, but if wrongly interpreted and applied, it serves the Devil's purpose to torment the sufferer further.

3. What was said was Wordy. "What have I said that makes you speak so endlessly?" (Job 16:3 TLB). "The ear groans at the quantity of windy talk, irrelevant observation, impertinent argument, and

pointless discussion to which it is obliged to listen." To say less than more is always safer and probably more effective.

4. What was said was Witless. Its abruptness, insensitivity, rashness, and pompousness were out of line. The words of the friends were "vain words" (Job 16:3), literally, "words of wind; words which pass by a man 'as the idle wind which he regards not.'" Unlike them, couch what is said based upon the promises of God, enveloped with sympathy and caring concern.

5. What was said was Wanting. Despite saying much, the friends failed to minister comfort and healing to Job's troubled heart. Their words were more wounding than soothing. Matthew Henry asserts, "Job desires his friends in imagination, for a little while, to change conditions with him, to put their souls in his soul's stead, to suppose themselves in misery like him and him at ease like them. Whatever our brethren's sorrows are, we ought by sympathy to make them our own because we know not how soon they may be so."[92]

"Sometimes we have to experience misunderstanding from unsympathetic friends in order to learn how to minister to others."[93]—Warren Wiersbe.

33

Simon Peter asked: "Lord, to whom shall we go?"

"Then Simon Peter answered Him, 'Lord, to whom shall we go?'" (John 6:68 KJ21). As others deserted Him, saying His teachings were "hard sayings," the disciples were asked by Jesus if they would also. Acting as their spokesman, Peter answered, saying, "Lord, to whom shall we go? Thou hast the words of eternal life. And we believe and are sure that thou art that Christ, the Son of the living God" (John 6:68–69).

"Lord, to whom shall we go?" for deliverance from sin and for forgiveness, if not to Thee? For consolation in sorrow, if not to

Thee? For meaning and purpose in life, if not to Thee? For peace and joy, if not to Thee? For escape from Hell and entrance to Heaven, if not to Thee? Where might these things be found, if not in Thee? The frank answer is in no one and nowhere.

> Where? O where?
> Where? O where?
> The poorest, the vilest, to Jesus may turn—
> Oh, where will you go if His mercy you spurn?
> –Wm. Stevenson (1884)

People who walk away from Christ go to a cistern that cannot remedy the problem of sin, satisfy the deep thirst and hunger of the soul, provide comfort and consolation in time of storm, grant meaning and happiness to life, or hope for Heaven at death (Jeremiah 2:13). To these, Jesus says, "Whoever drinks of the water that I shall give him will never thirst" (John 4:14 NKJV).

"If a man is saved, it is because God has saved him. But if a man is lost, that is to be attributed to his own rejection of the Gospel and his own rebellion against God's way of salvation."—Martyn Lloyd-Jones.

34

David asked: "And now, Lord, what wait I for?"

"And now, Lord, what wait I for? My hope is in thee" (Psalm 39:7). David, having pondered the shortness and uncertainty of life and its troubles and vexations, looks heavenward where his utmost hope is found in the Lord.[94]

The question is applicable to salvation. Man's nature is to delay salvation, to wait for something to occur before being saved.

1. Some people say they're waiting for God's time to be saved. I have good news. The waiting is over, for the time has arrived. The Bible says, "Behold, now is the accepted time! Behold, now is the day of salvation!" (2 Corinthians 6:2 KJ21).

2. Some say they're waiting on a sign to believe and be saved. Spurgeon asserts, "One has said to himself, 'If I had a dream, then I would believe.' Why, dear reader, do you crave signs and wonders? Isn't the Gospel its own sign and wonder? Isn't this the miracle of miracles, that 'God so loved the world, that he gave his only Son, that whoever believes in him should not perish'? Surely that precious word, 'Let the one who desires take the water of life without price,' and that solemn promise, 'Whoever comes to me I will never cast out,' are better than signs and wonders!"[95]

3. Others say they're waiting until they straighten their lives out. "Can the Ethiopian change his skin, or the leopard his spots?" (Jeremiah 13:23). Spurgeon answers, "The Ethiopian can wash or paint, but he cannot change that which is part and parcel of himself. A sinner cannot change his own nature."[96] He never will become fit for salvation.

4. Some say they're putting it off until later. Delay bears dangerous perils.

a. The peril of death. "Boast not thyself of tomorrow for thou knowest not what a day may bring forth" (Proverbs 27:1 JUB).

b. The peril of drifting further from Christ and the hardening of the heart toward Him (Hebrews 3:7–8).

c. The peril of God's wrath. "He, that being often reproved hardeneth his neck, shall suddenly be destroyed, and that without remedy" (Proverbs 29:1). "It is a fearful thing to fall into the hands of the living God" (Hebrews 10:31).

d. The peril of seeking Christ too late. The time to seek the Lord is "while He may be found" (Isaiah 55:6), indicating there will come a time when it's too late to seek Him. All of God's promises to the sinner are in the present tense.[97]

5. Some say they're waiting on the feeling. The only feeling necessary to be saved is a willingness to turn from sin and accept Christ as Lord and Savior. If a man will open the door to Christ that way, Christ promises to enter and save him (Revelation 3:20; John 1:12) regardless of the absence of blinding lights, earthquakes, or

the spiritual upheaval of the heart. Note, multitudes have died and gone to Hell, awaiting an unnecessary feeling that never came.

6. Others say they're waiting on better terms. It is foolish to believe that God will change the conditions of salvation to suit man's schedule and lifestyle. Sadly, some preachers and churches have altered the requirement for salvation without God's authority to man's eternal peril.

7. Some say they're waiting because they don't need to be Christians. The Bible makes clear that no man has the ability within himself to live life as it ought to be or to undo life's sins and mistakes that separate him from God. None who are sincere can say after reading the teachings of Jesus that they do not need to be Christians.[98]

"And now, Lord, what wait I for? My hope is in thee." With the psalmist, desist delay any longer. Place your hope for forgiveness, rightness with God, eternal life in Heaven, and peace and happiness not in a church, religion, possessions, morality, or good deeds, but in Christ alone. Say, "My hope from this moment forward is in Christ Jesus."

Christ receiveth sinful men,
  Even me with all my sin;
Purged from every spot and stain,
  Glory, I shall enter in.
–Erdmann Neumeister (1718)

"Tomorrow, you will have more sin to repent of. And tomorrow you will have a harder heart to repent with."[99]—Adrian Rogers.

35

Paul asked: "Lord, what wilt Thou have me to do?"

Paul's Damascus Road encounter with Christ convincingly proved to him that Christ was the Messiah, so much so that he asked,

"*Lord*, what wilt thou have me to do?" (Acts 9:6). It is a fitting question for the believer to ask. How might its answer be known?

1. Seek it. With Paul, pray, "Lord, what wilt thou have me to do?" with an unbiased heart. Sometimes, the believer predetermines the answer to prayer; the answer flows from his heart, not the throne of God. John Wesley said, "I find that the chief purpose in determining the will of God is to get my will in an unprejudiced state about the issue at hand."

2. Expect it. James cautions, "But let him ask in faith, never wavering; for he that wavereth is like a wave of the sea, driven and tossed by the wind. For let not that man think that he shall receive anything of the Lord" (James 1:6–7 KJ21).

3. Look for it. Man is prone to ask for knowledge of God's plan only to neglect to look for it and, therefore, not recognize it when it appears.

4. Wait for it. Chambers said, "One of the greatest strains in life is the strain of waiting for God." Don't waver in the waiting; wait until the Lord answers. "Wait, I say, on the Lord" (Psalm 27:14). Saith Spurgeon, "Wait in faith. Believe that though He keeps us tarrying, He will come at the right time and will not tarry."[100]

5. Verify it. F. B. Meyer said, "We have no right to ask for signs for the gratification of a morbid curiosity, but we are justified in asking for the concurrence of outward providence indicating the will of God." Another says, "It is a vital principle of the Lord's guidance for a Christian never to move from the spot where he is sure God has placed him until the 'pillar of cloud' (Exodus 13:21) moves."[101] It's okay to step back and ask God to confirm what you believe to be His will and plan.

6. Accept it. Success awaits him who submits to the plan. Maclaren counsels, "Be quite willing to accept it [divine guidance], whether the finger points down the broad road that we would like to

go upon, or through some tangled path amongst the brushwood that we would fain avoid."

An old Scottish woman sold thread, buttons, and shoestrings in country homes. At an unmarked crossroad, she would toss a stick in the air and go in the direction it pointed when it fell to the ground. One day, she was seen tossing the stick into the air three times. "Why did you toss the stick several times?" someone asked.

She answered, "It has pointed every time to the road going to the right, and I want to go on the road to the left. It looks smoother!" Relentlessly, the woman kept throwing up the stick until it pointed toward the road she wanted to take. Note, don't keep tossing the stick into the air when God points in the direction to go. Don't trade a difficult or undesirable road that is God's will for one that is easier and preferred, which is not. God will guide us to and down the path we are to travel, provided we yield ourselves to His control.

"The one supreme business of life is to find God's plan for your life and live it. Learn to take no steps apart from God's direction."—E. Stanley Jones.

36

The Disciples asked: "Why could not we cast him out?"

"And when He had come into the house, His disciples asked Him privately, 'Why could not we cast him out?' And He said unto them, 'This kind can come forth by nothing but by prayer and fasting'" (Mark 9:28–29 KJ21). Unexpectedly, a father brought his demon-possessed son to the disciples for an exorcism. But "they could not" help him (Mark 9:18). Jesus healed the boy. Later inside the house the disciples "asked him [Jesus] privately, why could not we cast him out?" (Mark 9:28). Jesus answered, "This kind can come forth by nothing, but by prayer and fasting" (Mark 9:29). But they didn't have time to fast and pray at that moment. It happened too quickly. And that's the point. They should have been "prayed up" to face such an unexpected ministry opportunity with God's power. Note, Christians must always maintain battle readiness.

1. Readiness to minister takes faith. "All things are possible to him that believeth" (Mark 9:23). Faith taps the power of God to do what impotent and feeble men cannot. The disciples were rebuked for their lack of faith in Jesus' ability to use them to help the demon-possessed boy (Matthew 17:20). The rebuke teaches that faith can be increased, developed, and grown. How? Paul answers, "So then faith cometh by hearing, and hearing by the word of God" (Romans 10:17). Additionally, it is fostered by communion with the Lord. "Lord, I believe; help Thou mine unbelief" (Mark 9:24). Simeon said, "Only go forth in faith, and all the Goliaths in the universe shall fall under your hand."[102]

2. Readiness to minister takes prayer. Deficiency in prayer results in a power deficiency (Mark 9:29).[103] The disciples should have been better "prayed up." Chrysostom said, "The potency of prayer hath subdued the strength of fire; it has bridled the rage of lions, hushed anarchy to rest, extinguished wars, appeased the elements, expelled demons, burst the chains of death, expanded the gates of Heaven, assuaged diseases, dispelled frauds, rescued cities from destruction, stayed the sun in its course, and arrested the progress of the thunderbolt."[104] Barclay asserts, "God may have given us a gift, but unless we maintain close contact with Him, it may wither and die."[105]

3. Readiness to minister takes fasting (Mark 9:29). The fast is a period without food or pleasure, spent earnestly seeking God's face for power, renewal, a blessing, or a need. Its ultimate purpose, says Thrasher, is to be "separated to the Lord and to concentrate on godliness."[106] Could the neglect of the fast be, at least partially, responsible for the feebleness and weakness of the church to impact the escalating evil and the multitudes shackled to sin?

These three things—faith, prayer, and fasting—will enable believers to triumph over Satan.

"How important it is to stay spiritually fresh; you never know when somebody may need your help."[107]—Warren Wiersbe.

37

The disciples asked: "Who then can be saved?"

"When His disciples heard it, they were exceedingly amazed, saying, 'Who then can be saved?'" (Matthew 19:25 KJ21). What prompted the disciples' question was the words of Jesus, "It is hard for a rich man to enter the kingdom of Heaven."

"Who then can be saved?"

1. None, on their terms. To be saved, a man must come on God's terms, not a church's or his own. Spurgeon remarks, "You undeserving mortals dream that my Lord is to be dictated to by you! You are beggars at His gate asking for mercy, and you are drawing up rules and regulations as to how He will give that mercy. Do you think that He will submit to this?"[108]

2. None, by their efforts. Jonathan Edwards said, "You contribute nothing to your salvation except the sin that made it necessary." The mighty gulf caused by sin between God and man cannot be bridged through man's religious works, keeping of the Ten Commandments, or moral goodness. Paul said, "He saved us because of his mercy, not because of good deeds we did to be right with God" (Titus 3:5 ICB).

3. None, by their associations. God has no stepchildren. No person enters the kingdom of God on the coattails of another's faith.

4. None, by their power. Matthew Henry says, "The wisdom of man would soon be nonplussed in contriving, and the power of man baffled in effecting, the salvation of a soul. No creature can work the change necessary to the salvation of a soul, either in itself or in anyone else."[109]

5. None, by their religion. Church membership or religious rites, ordinances, and sacraments cannot forgive sin and save the soul.

6. None, against their will. President Andrew Jackson offered a pardon to George Wilson on death row. The man refused the amnesty. Supreme Court Justice John Marshall declared, "The value of the pardon depends upon its acceptance. If it is refused, then there is no pardon." Mr. Mitchell died on the gallows. The same is true concerning the pardon God extends to the condemned sinner.

Who then can be saved? Regardless of a person's vileness, all who meet God's conditions of belief, confession, repentance, and placement of faith in Christ may be saved (Romans 10:9–13).

"Those who are thoroughly convinced of sin and truly concerned about their salvation will give themselves up to Christ."—Matthew Henry.

38

The People asked: "Who is this son of man?"

"The people answered Him,…'Who is this son of man?'" (John 12:34 KJ21). Jesus' discourse about the death He would die puzzled the crowd; they thought Messiah would live forever. They asked how Jesus could say the Son of Man would die and who He was.

"Who is this son of man?"

1. It is a question compelled by Christ's sinless life. Of Christ, Pilate said, "I find no fault in Him." Of His enemies, Jesus asked, "Which of you convicts me of sin?" (John 8:46 RSV). None brought any accusation forward. "He committed no sin, neither was deceit found in his mouth" (1 Peter 2:22 ESV). Strauss said, "Jesus had a conscience unclouded by the memory of sin." How was Jesus able to do what no man can do—to live without sin? He is the Son of God.

2. It is a question compelled by Christ's claim to be the Messiah. Christ asserted that He existed before Abraham and was the Jehovah of the Old Testament (John 8:56–59). He declared Himself to be the only Way or Door to Heaven (John 14:6; 10:9) and that "my kingdom is not of this world" (John 18:36). He asserted, "I and my Father are one" (John 10:30). When pressed whether or not He was the Son of God, the Messiah, and the Son of Man (Mark 14:61–64), He affirmed that He was. A. T. Robertson remarks of that assertion, "Jesus accepts the challenge and admits that He claims to be all three. 'Ye say' is just a Greek idiom for yes (compare 'I AM' in Mark 14:62 with 'Thou hast said' in Matthew 26:64)."

3. It is a question compelled by the miracles Christ performed. The miracles of Christ are documented in Scripture and external sources such as the *Acts of Pontius Pilate*, the testimony of the Jewish historian Josephus, and the Sanhedrin, Jesus' enemies. R. C. Sproul wrote, "They [genuine miracles] and they alone ultimately prove that Christ is the Son of God and that the Bible is the Word of God. All other 'evidence' is corroborative."[110]

4. It is a question compelled by Christ's virgin birth. Isaiah prophesized 700 years before the birth of Jesus that Messiah would be conceived of a virgin (Isaiah 7:14). Christ's immaculate conception leading to His birth in the manger at Bethlehem reveals that He is the promised Messiah, the Son of God who came to earth on a redemptive mission. Adrian Rogers says, "Jesus is not the Son of God because He was born of a virgin—He was born of a virgin because He is the Son of God."[111]

5. It is a question compelled by Christ's substitutionary death. Saith Criswell, "The death of Christ provides the propitiation [cancellation of sin's effect] for the sins of the whole world. Men may reject the Lord's substitutionary death, accepting condemnation instead, but Jesus died for all."[112]

6. It is a question compelled by Christ's resurrection. "And declared to be the Son of God with power, according to the spirit of

holiness, by the resurrection from the dead" (Romans 1:4). There is a preponderance of evidence for Christ's resurrection. Note that Jesus attested that His resurrection would be the pivotal proof of His deity (Matthew 28:6).

7. It is a question compelled by the Holy Scriptures. The Bible says, "For in him [Christ] the whole fullness of deity dwells bodily, and you have been filled in him, who is the head of all rule and authority" (Colossians 2:9–10 ESV). Saith Oswald Sanders, "The deity of Christ is the key doctrine of the Scriptures. Reject it, and the Bible becomes a jumble of words without any unifying theme. Accept it, and the Bible becomes an intelligible and ordered revelation of God in the person of Jesus Christ." A. W. Pink says, "Certainty that Christ is 'the Son of the living God' comes not by listening to the labored arguments of seminary professors, nor by studying books on Christian evidence, but by believing what God has said about His Son in the Holy Scriptures."[113]

"Who is this son of man?" It is a question whose answer allows only one answer: Either Jesus is the Son of God as He claimed, or else He is a liar, lunatic, or something worse.[114] Considering the irrefutable facts about Christ and the testimony of Scripture, the question must be answered by saying, "Thou art the Christ, the son of the living God" (Matthew 16:16).

"To be a Christian indeed is sincerely to believe that Jesus is the Christ, and to act accordingly."[115]—Matthew Henry.

39

Malachi asked: "Who can endure the day of his coming?"

"But who can endure the day of his coming, and who can stand when he appears? For he is like a refiner's fire and like fullers' soap" (Malachi 3:2 MEV). Malachi seems to blend prophecies of the first and second coming of Christ. With the first coming, Christ will provide the means of repentance to escape judgment; with the second coming, His judgment will be without remedy.

The fact of Christ's first coming is documented. His return is what believers now joyously anticipate. Much, but far from all, of that event is stated in the Scripture.

1. The certainty of it. The Bible overwhelmingly substantiates the return of Christ and provides it with credible documentation. By a ratio of eight to one, references to the Second Coming of Christ in the Bible outnumber those to the First Coming. Criswell asserts, "There is no truth more certain in the entire Bible than the personal, literal, and imminent return of the Lord Jesus Christ."[116] Francis Dixon says, "Scripture knows no first coming without a second coming. The two comings are entwined, interwoven, and inseparable in the prophetic Word."[117]

2. The manner of it. Paul says, "For the Lord himself shall descend from heaven with a shout, with the voice of the archangel, and with the trump of God: and the dead in Christ shall rise first: Then we which are alive and remain shall be caught up together with them in the clouds, to meet the Lord in the air: and so shall we ever be with the Lord" (1 Thessalonians 4:16–17). When the Bible speaks of the Second Coming of Christ, it does not refer to the coming of the Holy Spirit or His coming in the sinner's salvation or coming for the saint at death. It addresses the physical and visible bodily return of Christ to take the redeemed of God to their Home in Heaven. The angels said to the watching disciples, "This same Jesus, who is taken up from you into Heaven, shall so come in like manner as ye have seen Him go into Heaven" (Acts 1:11 KJ21).

3. The time of it. "Who can endure *the day* of his coming?" Malachi speaks of a specific date or time for Christ's return, known only to God (Matthew 24:36). It will occur suddenly. Paul says it will happen, "In a moment, in the twinkling of an eye" (1 Corinthians 15:52). Jesus describes that day: "Two men will be in the field; one will be taken and the other left. Two women will be grinding with a hand mill; one will be taken and the other left. Therefore keep watch, because you do not know on what day your Lord will come" (Matthew 24:40–42 NIV).

4. The preparation for it. Malachi inquires, "*Who can endure the day of his coming?*" It is a consequential question. Who will be able to stand accepted and justified at his coming? Not the hypocrite, the Christian in name only. Not the worldly, whose god is the pleasures and possessions of the world. Not the religionist, who bases salvation upon good works and personal goodness. Not the unbeliever who rejects the notion of Christ and the cross.

Who then can abide on the day of his coming? The man who by faith has embraced Christ as Lord and Savior and walks with Him in devoted fellowship. Note, if unregenerate, receive Christ into your life without delay or procrastination as Lord and Savior.

"To me, the second coming is the perpetual light on the path which makes the present bearable. This is now His Word to all believing souls: 'Till I come.' We are not looking for death; we are looking for Him."[118]—G. Campbell Morgan.

40

Moses asked: "What doth the Lord thy God require of thee?"

"And now, Israel, what doth the Lord thy God require of thee, but to fear the Lord thy God, to walk in all His ways, and to love Him, and to serve the Lord thy God with all thy heart and with all thy soul, To keep the commandments of the LORD, and his statutes, which I command thee this day for thy good?" (Deuteronomy 10:12–13).

"What doth the Lord thy God require of thee?"

1. To fear Him. To fear the Lord is not to be terrified of Him but to manifest holy awe, submission, and reverence for Him.

2. To obey Him. To walk in the ways of the Lord is to follow the path of righteousness, holiness, and truth. It is to walk in accord with His plan and will.

3. To love Him. To love the Lord "with all thy heart and with all thy soul" is to express affection and allegiance to Him above all

others. The best witness for Christ is duty based on love for Him, not reward or man's applause. Jesus said, "If ye love me, keep my commandments" (John 14:15). "Perform all he prescribes; forbear all the forbids."[119]

4. To serve Him. MacArthur states, "To serve the Lord is 'to have the worship of the Lord as the central focus of life.'"[120]

Of these requirements, note:

1. They are sacred. Sovereign God, not man, gave them and therefore ought to be obeyed (Deuteronomy 10:14).

2. They are reasonable. "Which is your reasonable service" (Romans 12:1). Matthew Henry says, "When we have received mercy from God, it becomes us to enquire what returns we shall make to Him. Consider what He requires, and you will find it is nothing but what is highly just and reasonable in itself and of unspeakable benefit and advantage to you."[121]

3. They are beneficial. "To keep the commandments of the LORD and His statutes which I command thee this day *for thy good.*" Simon says, "You cannot but acknowledge that everything which God requires of you is both good in itself and conducive to your greatest good."[122]

"The most joyful people in this world are those who know God as their loving Heavenly Father and who seek to do those things which He asks of them, for their own good and for His glory."[123]—Francis Dixon.

41

David asked: "Wherewithal shall a young man cleanse his way?"

"Wherewithal shall a young man cleanse his way?" (Psalm 119:9). Of life's many questions for youth, few rise any higher than David's. How might a youth be made clean from the defilement of sin and its addictiveness to live a morally pure life?

The unadulterated Word of God, its doctrines, teachings, warnings, and examples 'hid in the heart' and habitually heeded perform a three-fold work.

1. The Word points out sin. Paul said, "It was the law that showed me my sin. I would never have known the sin in my heart—the evil desires that are hidden there—if the law had not said, 'You must not have evil desires in your heart'" (Romans 7:7 TLB). MacArthur asserts, "The law [Ten Commandments] reveals the divine standard, and as believers compare themselves against that standard, they can accurately identify sin, which is the failure to meet the standard."[124] God's Word is a mirror that reveals sin inwardly and outwardly. Stored in the heart, it is like a referee in a football game. When an infraction of the rules occurs, it signals it by tossing a yellow flag and blowing a screeching whistle in the offender's conscience.

2. The Word purges sin. God's Word exposes sin and then prompts its renunciation and expulsion by confession and repentance (2 Timothy 3:16–17).

3. The Word prevents sin. It is the cleanest "Book" and will enable the person who embraces and obeys it to be clean (James 1:22–25). MacArthur says, "Internalizing the Word is a believer's best weapon to defend against encroaching sin."[125] The Word 'hid in the heart' secures it against the influence of Satan, heresy, worldliness, and sin.

Gill states, "The word of God is a most powerful antidote against sin, when it has a place in the heart; not only the precepts of it forbid sin, but the promises of it influence and engage to the purity of heart and life."[126] Spurgeon advises, "Young man, the Bible must be your chart, and you must exercise great watchfulness that your way may be according to its directions."[127] Simeon says, "A mariner may be drawn from his course by currents, as well as driven by winds; and therefore, from day to day, he consults his compass and his chart to see whether there has been any deviation from his destined path. The same precautions must be used by you."[128] Someone said the Bible will keep you from sin, and sin will keep you from the Bible.

The bottom-line. How is a young man triumphant over the evil of the day? Benson says, "By diligently and circumspectly watching over himself, and examining and regulating all his dispositions and actions by the rule of Thy word."[129] The Bible will keep you from sin; sin will keep you from the Bible.

"The ruin of young men is either living at large (or by no rule at all) or choosing to themselves false rules; let them ponder the path of their feet, and walk by Scripture rules so their way shall be clean, and they shall have the comfort and credit of it here and forever."[130]—Matthew Henry.

42

Gehazi asked: "Is it well with you?"

"Run now, I pray thee, to meet her and say unto her, 'Is it well with thee?'…And she answered, 'It is well'" (2 Kings 4:26 KJ21). The only child (a son, maybe three or four years old) of a Shunammite mother suddenly fell ill in the morning while with his father playing in the field among the reapers and was dead at noon. Upon Gehazi's question, asked on behalf of Elisha, "Is it well with thee?" she, by faith, answered, "It is well" with the child.

What constitutes a person saying it is well with them? It is not that they are merely in good health. It is not that they possess silver and gold. It is not that they have sufficient food, shelter, and clothing. It is not that they have been baptized and attend church. Note, for things to be well for a man, all must be well with his soul presently and eternally. It is well with a man if his sins are forgiven, if he has been passed from death unto life, if Christ is cherished and treasured, if he walks in compliance with Christ's teaching and rules—if fellowship with Christ is constantly maintained (Isaiah 3:10).

What is your answer to the question? Is it well with you? Are you born-again? Have you forsaken all to follow Christ? Do you walk righteously? Is Christ loved with all the heart, soul, mind, and strength? Is Christ the joy of your life? Do you value a relationship with Christ above all others? How these questions are answered indicates the answer to Elisha's question, "Is it well with you?"

"O beloved, if God declares that all is well, ten thousand devils may declare it to be ill, but we laugh them all to scorn."[131]—C. H. Spurgeon.

43

Phillip asked: "Understandest thou what thou readest?"

"And Philip ran thither to him, and heard him reading the prophet Isaiah, and said, 'Understandest thou what thou readest?' And he said, 'How can I, unless some man should guide me?'" (Acts 8:30–31 KJ21). Prompted by the Holy Spirit, Philip engaged an Ethiopian Eunuch about his understanding of the Scripture, which led to his conversion.

Note four lessons drawn from the narrative.

1. The Word is not understood for various reasons.

 a. It lacks a spiritual foundation necessary for its comprehension (the rudiments or ABCs of the faith).

 b. Man's unregenerate estate. Paul says, "The natural man receiveth not the things of the Spirit of God: for they are foolishness unto him: neither can he know them, because they are spiritually discerned" (1 Corinthians 2:14). At conversion, the Bible becomes a brand-new book read with new eyes.

 c. A wrong approach. Reading the Word to bend it to fit personal beliefs and preferences or to pick out mistakes and errors is futile.

 d. Fragmentary facts. Sound theology is based on Scripture as a unit of Truth, not texts taken out of context.

2. The Word is meant to be understood. There is no better question than, "What saith the Scriptures?" How can people understand it?

 a. Through its Author. Ask the Holy Spirit, who inspired the Bible, to grant understanding of it. A wind chime is a silent instrument until placed where the wind blows upon it—it then gives forth a clanking sound. The Bible is silent until the breath of the Holy

Spirit blows upon it, causing it to sound forth "wonderful words of life." "Speak, LORD, for Thy servant heareth."

b. Through conservative commentaries and books.

c. Through biblically sound teachers and friends. Phillip aided the Eunuch, and Apollos received the help of Aquila and Priscilla. When asked why he had such incredible knowledge, a Persian philosopher answered, "By not allowing shame to prevent me from asking questions when I was ignorant." Humble yourself and ask questions of godly, learned men. Note that mature saints proficient in the Scriptures ought to help those who lack understanding.

d. Through meditation. Some truths may only be understood by wrestling long and hard with them, not glancing briefly at them. David said, "While I was musing, the fire burned" (Psalm 39:3 KJ21). Spurgeon advises, "Have the crackers with you to crack the nuts, that you may feed upon their kernels. When you read a passage which you do not understand, read it until you do."[132]

3. Understanding the Word is of paramount importance. Time spent in the Word is never wasted. Why? It instructs in the way of forgiveness and salvation and Heaven. It teaches the way to happiness, meaning in life, and hope. "Study this Book of Instruction continually. Meditate on it day and night so you will be sure to obey everything written in it. Only then will you prosper and succeed in all you do" (Joshua 1:8 NLT).

4. The Word is profitable even when not understood. No man can read it without being impacted by it. Fortunately, the Eunuch kept reading it despite not understanding it, which prepared his heart for Phillip's witness and resulted in his salvation and baptism. Faith is birthed from reading and hearing the Word of God (Romans 10:17). Never quit reading it out of a lack of understanding. "For the word of God is alive and active. Sharper than any double-edged sword, it penetrates even to dividing soul and spirit, joints and marrow; it judges the thoughts and attitudes of the heart" (Hebrews 4:12 NIV).

"What we read and hear of the Word of God highly concerns us to understand, especially what we read and hear concerning

Christ; therefore, we should often ask ourselves whether we understand it or not."[133]—Matthew Henry.

44

Scoffers asked: "Where is the promise of his coming?"

Having seen no signs of Christ's return, scoffers mocked the claim, saying, "Where is the promise of his coming?" (2 Peter 3:4). Mockingly, they said that the promise had failed.

"Where is the promise of His coming?" It is found in prophetic Scripture, the testimony of the saints, and the words of Christ.

1. The declaration of Prophetic Scripture. Scholars say that the prophecy of the Second Coming is mentioned at least 1,200 times in the Old Testament[134] and found in at least seventeen books. In the New Testament, there are 318 references that directly or indirectly refer to it: one verse in every thirty and seven out of every ten chapters. Daniel prophesied about it (Daniel 7:13–14). Enoch testified of it (Jude 14–15). Isaiah declared it, describing the peace on earth under His rule (Isaiah 11:1–10). The psalmist pronounced it: "For he comes, for he comes to judge the earth" (Psalm 96:13 ESV). Zechariah taught it (Zechariah 14:3–9).

2. The testimony of the Saints. Paul believed it (1 Thessalonians 4:16–17). The Gospels teach it. The Olivet Discourse vividly and explicitly describes the Second Coming of Christ (Matthew 24–25; Mark 13; Luke 21:5–38). The author of Hebrews emphasized it (Hebrews 9:28). James affirmed it (James 5:7–8). Peter asserts it (1 Peter 5:4). John amplifies it (1 John 3:2). The Book of Revelation, authored by John, reveals it. Revelation 19 explicitly details that glorious event.

3. The words of Christ. Jesus unquestionably and dogmatically asserts that He will return. In John 14, the promise is stated in four words: "I will come back" (John 14:3 GNT). In Revelation 22, the promise of Christ's return is said three times in three verses, "Behold, I come quickly" (verse 7), "Behold, I come quickly" (verse 12), "Surely I come quickly" (verse 20). In John 16 He said, "In a

little while you will see Me no more, and then after a little while you will see Me" (John 16:16 NIV). Christ spoke of His return 21 times.

Criswell asserts, "The infallibility, integrity, and moral authority of the Son of God are bound up in His keeping that word that He will come again."[135] And He will. Christ's word is dependable and trustworthy. What He says always happens. Of His Second Advent, He stated, "If it were not so, I would have told you." "God is not a man, that he should lie" (Numbers 23:19).

Despite scoffers and mockers of the Second Coming, as in Peter's Day (2 Peter 3:3), the evidence is overwhelming. Christ will come to take His children Home to Heaven (2 Peter 3:10). That is unalterable. "Look up, and lift up your heads; for your redemption draweth nigh" (Luke 21:28). Saith Spurgeon, "Brethren and sisters, regard the object of our expectations! See the happiness which is promised us! Behold the Heaven which awaits us! Forget for a while your present cares; let all your difficulties and your sorrows vanish for a season, and live for a while in the future which is so certified by faithful promises that you may rejoice in it even now!"[136]

"There is no truth more certain in the entire Bible."—W. A. Criswell.

45

Paul asked: "O death, where is thy sting?"

"O death, where is thy sting [power to hurt]? O grave, where is thy victory?" (1 Corinthians 15:55).

The venomous sting of sin, which gave death its power, Christ disarmed and destroyed by His death and resurrection. Says Matthew Henry, "It may hiss, therefore, but it cannot hurt. Death may seize a believer but cannot sting him or hold him in his power."[137] Death no longer has a final say-so about our bodies and eternal estate. Jesus said, "I am the resurrection and the Life. He that believeth in Me, though he were dead, yet shall he live" (John 11:25 KJ21). Lenski writes, "Death and all of its apparent victories are undone for God's children. What looks like a victory for death and like a defeat for us when our bodies die and decay shall be utterly reversed so that death dies in absolute defeat and our bodies live again in absolute victory."[138] Hallelujah!

A boy highly allergic to bee stings became terrified when a bee flew in the car window. The father stopped the car, allowing the boy to escape while he captured the bee. Back in the car, the boy, seeing the bee and hearing it buzz, cried out with fear again. The boy's fear calmed when the father opened his hand, revealing the bee's stinger. Death makes a lot of fuss and noise but is powerless to harm the believer, for Jesus Christ bore its stinger upon the cross.

There's a lot of bothersome, disturbing noise about death that the Devil orchestrates toward the dying saint. But that's all it is, just noise. And the noise has never hurt anyone. Despite all the Devil does to create fear and anxiety about death, it is quickly dispelled by faith in God and His promises. Fear of stepping into the unknown at death is thwarted, for we know Heaven awaits. Fear about parting from family and friends subsides, for we know they will be seen again. Fear and guilt for things done are appeased, for we know our sins are forgiven. Fear of punishment in Hell is removed, for Christ has secured our eternal deliverance from it.

A terror-smitten conscience stings over its reproach and transgression of God's law, guilt, and day of accountability that will result in the darkness and torment of Hell forever. We once knew such a sting and pain, but now they are gone. "Thanks be to God, who giveth us the victory through our Lord Jesus Christ!" (1 Corinthians 15:57 ASV).

"Death is left stingless to all who believe and accept Him."[139]— J. Vaughan.

46

Paul asked: "Who shall separate us from the love of Christ?"

"Who shall separate us from the love of Christ?" (Romans 8:35). The answer is no one or nothing. In Romans 8:38–39, Paul enumerates seven clusters of things that cannot sever Christ's love [saving relationship] from the believer.

1. The first "cluster" of things Paul states that cannot separate the saint from Christ are the troubles of life (tribulation, distress, hunger, and being destitute—lack of sufficient clothing). Calamities do not remove but rather serve to prove the steadfast love of Christ to His children. He never "abandons ship" despite the fierceness of the storm or the impoverishment of life.

2. The second cluster of things that cannot divorce the saint from Christ is the hostility of man (persecution, danger, and the sword). The saint may be deprived of food and water, stripped of earthly possessions, cast into a rat-infested prison, tormented heinously, and thrust through with a sword for the cause of the Gospel. Still, Christ's companionship and compassion can never be killed or taken away.

3. The third cluster of things that cannot remove the love of Christ from the saint is the unseen powers of Heaven and Hell (angels, God's Heavenly army, principalities, Satan, and demons). Witmer says, "Angels would not, and demons could not undo God's relationship with His redeemed ones."[140] All the battalions of Hell combined are unable to divorce Christ and His love from the redeemed.

4. The fourth cluster of things that cannot sever the love of Christ from the saint are the two sides of existence (life and death). The love of Christ is not bound to life but extends into death (Romans 14:8).

5. The fifth cluster of things that cannot shake the love of Christ from the saint are the extremes of time (things present and things to come).[141] The hardships, infirmity, sorrow, or suffering experienced now and whatever may be experienced tomorrow cannot thwart the love of Christ one iota.

6. The sixth cluster of things that cannot deprive the saint of the love of Christ are the powers in space (height and depth). Happenings in space above or below the horizon cannot sever the believer's relationship to Christ.[142]

7. The seventh and final cluster of things that cannot injure the love of Christ for the saint are the forces in the created world (powers and "any other created thing"). Paul underscores, for the second time, the impotence of the host of Hell to sever the love of Christ from the saint. Just as incompetent for that task is any government antagonistic to the Christian. "Any other created thing" comprehensively includes anything that Paul may have omitted among the things that cannot defeat the love of Christ in the saint ("personal or impersonal, animate or inanimate, known or unknown"[143]). "Many waters cannot drown His love, nor the floods quench it."[144]

What fabulous assurance the saint possesses about the certainty of Christ's ever-present love, guardianship, and help. Nothing is more sure and secure than personal salvation wrought and preserved by Christ. Come what may, the love of Christ for you is unshakable, immoveable, and changeless. Hath he not said, "I have graven thee upon the palms of my hands." "The mountains shall depart, and the hills be removed; but my kindness shall not depart from thee, neither shall the covenant of my peace be removed, saith the Lord that hath mercy on thee?" (Isaiah 49:16; 54:10).

"Christ does not love you today and cast you away tomorrow."[145]—C. H. Spurgeon.

47

The Samaritan woman asked: "From whence then hast thou that living water?"

"Jesus answered and said unto her, 'If thou knewest the gift of God and who it is that saith to thee, "Give Me to drink," thou wouldest have asked of Him, and He would have given thee living water.' The woman said unto Him, 'Sir, thou hast nothing to draw with, and the well is deep. From whence then hast thou that living water?'" (John 4:10–11).

From start to end, John details how Jesus won the woman at Jacob's well to saving faith (John 4:6–25).

Step One. Jesus saw her as a sinner in need of salvation. The woman's water jug was full, but her heart was empty. See people as He saw her: empty souls thirsting for hope, healing, and happiness.

Step Two. He refused to allow her sinful lifestyle or the racial prejudice that existed between the Jews and the Samaritans to hinder the witness. Soulwinning crosses every barrier to bring man to God.

Step Three. Jesus engages the woman by requesting water to drink. Requests and questions help initiate the gospel witness.

Step Four. Jesus connects the woman's need for salvation with the well from which she was drawing water. The physical was used to preach the spiritual.

Step Five. He kept the witness simple. Jesus knew all the theological lingo but shelved it to share the Gospel in a way the woman could comprehend. All men are like little children in their understanding of the gospel message. Keep the cookies on the bottom shelf.

Step Six. Jesus skillfully unmasked her sin and confronted it. Tactfully, the soulwinner must point to sin, its consequences, and only remedy (Romans 3:23; 6:23).

Step Seven. He was prepared to handle her opposing theological views and objections. The soulwinner must be ready to thwart religious misconceptions and flawed theology (1 Peter 3:15).

Step Eight. Jesus refused to be sidetracked by the woman's questions. He turned her questions into a springboard to drive the gospel message home to her heart. In witnessing, always "wrestle" the conversation back to the person's need from secondary issues they may raise.

Step Nine. Jesus listened to the woman. Soulwinners are good listeners. Listening provides insight into the person's misconceptions about salvation (as it did to Jesus about this woman), spiritual knowledge, and difficulties with becoming a Christian.

Step Ten. Jesus did not compromise the message. She must drink of the living waters (salvation) offered to be saved. No alternative was offered.

Step Eleven. Jesus cited how the means of salvation could be received. "Thou wouldest have asked." It must be requested in prayer by faith. Through prayer, man accesses Christ to forgive sin and salvation (the sinner's prayer).

Step Twelve. Jesus gave His best effort to win the woman. Soulwinning is absorbent, wholehearted work (John 4:34).[146] He didn't hold back but spoke to her like she was the only lost soul on earth. Make each witness the best possible.

Step Thirteen. Jesus drew the net. Upon allowing the woman to respond to the gospel presentation, she was gloriously saved at the first asking. End a witness with an invitation to be saved (apart from coercion) "then and there." Note, evidence of the woman's conversion is manifest in the bold witness she made to the people of the city (John 4:29) that caused many to believe (John 4:39). Roland Leavell states, "When a man meets Christ, he learns to love souls."[147] This woman did. All do.

"**Jesus has everything in perfect readiness so soon as the heart begins to feel its thirst.**"[148]—D. Young.

48

James asked: "Is any sick among you?"

"Is any sick among you?" (James 5:14). James gives instructions to the saints as to what to do when sick, feeble, and weak (James 5:14–15). "Let him pray." The afflicted are to pray for relief or recovery based upon the will of God (James 5:16). Criswell says, "This above everything else: when I am sick, let me take myself to God. Let me take myself to God."[149]

"Let him call." The sickly (not just the ailing but defeated, feeble, and weary warrior) may invite the "elders" to visit and pray for them. The act is entirely voluntary. "For the elders." Elders are spiritually mature leaders in the church who have been divinely appointed and qualified by the Holy Spirit to have "the spiritual care of and to exercise oversight over the church" (the shepherds, the overseers of the flock—1 Peter 5:1–2).[150]

"Let them pray over him." Barnes suggests that elders pray "that relief from pain may be granted, that the mind may be calm and submissive, that the medicines employed may be blessed to a restoration to health [if per God's divine will], that past sins may be forgiven, that he who is sick may be sanctified by his trials, that he may be restored to health [if in agreement with God's will] or prepared for his 'last change' [transition to Glory]."[151]

"Anointing him with oil." While prayer is the *primary* function, it is to be accompanied by oil, whose purpose is medicinal. The two combined denote the elder's role in aiding a person's physical and spiritual needs.[152] The oil rubbed into a wound in Paul's day brought comfort and promoted healing.[153] All evangelicals agree that the anointing with oil bears no magic healing power.

"In Jesus' name." To pray in Jesus' name is to pray in accordance with His divine will. It is praying that recovery or restoration will occur "if it be thy will." "And the prayer of faith." It is crystal clear that the prayer of faith, not the anointing with oil, is the means of healing or restoration when it is God's will to grant it.[154] The absence of healing doesn't mean a lack of faith. Paul, with great faith, prayed for healing, which never came. Paul's valued friend and helper, Trophimus, was sick, yet Paul's faith did not heal him. Moses pleaded with God, 'O God, let me live, let me go into the land with these people' (Deuteronomy 3:25). And yet he died. Hezekiah pleaded for additional years, and he lived (Isaiah 38:5).

Healing is contingent upon what God counts best for the person and His glory. Shadrach, Meshach, and Abednego facing the burning furnace, said, "Our God is able to deliver us" (Daniel 3:17 TLB). They didn't say He *would* deliver them. They trusted Him to do what was best, whether He did or not. This is the right attitude and approach to healing. Faith says we can always trust God's judgment to do what is expedient regarding our health.

"Call out to God for help. Will He do what you want? I cannot say, but this I can say: He will do what is best."[155]—Max Lucado.

49

Martha asked: "Dost thou not care that my sister hath left me to serve alone?"

"Martha was encumbered with much serving, and came to Him and said, 'Lord, dost Thou not care that my sister hath left me to serve alone? Bid her therefore that she help me.'" And Jesus answered and said unto her, "Martha, Martha, thou art anxious and troubled about many things. But one thing is needful, and Mary hath chosen that good part'" (Luke 10:38–42).

Martha's fault was not in the service performed for the Lord. It is the duty of all saints to labor for Christ. Her fault was not even in her "much serving." Believers must do as much as they can for Christ.[156] Martha's fault was that Christ got lost in all the hustle and bustle of service. She allowed service to eclipse the need for communion. Spurgeon says, "See to it that sitting at the Savior's feet is not neglected, even though it is under the specious pretext of doing Him service."[157] Note, "If the enemy can distract you from your time alone with God, then he can isolate you from the help that comes from God alone."[158]

The ideal is a combination of Mary and Martha's spirit. Spend time in sweet communion with Christ, feeding the soul and filling the fountain of the soul, and then serve Him zealously as commissioned. Spurgeon states, "To catch the Spirit of Christ, to be filled with Himself, this will equip us for godly labor as nothing else ever can."[159] Note that being a Martha at work is far easier than being a Mary at worship. Satan battles time spent with Christ more rigorously than that done for Him.

"The closet first, the study and activities second, both study and activities freshened and made efficient by the closet."[160]—E. M. Bounds.

50
Moses asked: "Who is on the Lord's side?"

"Then Moses stood in the gate of the camp, and said, who is on the Lord's side? Let him come unto me. And all the sons of Levi gathered themselves together unto him" (Exodus 32:26). With the Ten Commandments in hand, Moses discovers the people worshipping a golden calf at the foot of Sinai. Shocked and saddened, he asks the question of the text.

What is it to be on the Lord's side? It is to align oneself with Christ wholly and devotedly (the New Birth), the Holy Scriptures (the Standard by which man is to live), the New Testament church, the saints, and His kingdom cause (boldly rebuking sin, testifying of the truth, and saturating the land with the good news of the Gospel).

Note, no man is automatically on Christ's side. Simeon says, "By nature, we are all 'enemies to God,' and 'children of wrath.' It is by grace alone that our state can be changed so that we can, with justice, be numbered as the servants of the Lord."[161]

"Who is on the Lord's side? Let him come unto me."

1. It is a divine question. Not Moses, but God asks it of every man; therefore, give it the utmost consideration.

2. It is a dominant question. It rises above every other question, urging immediate response. No more excellent or pressing question faces a person.

3. It is a determinate question. Man's good or evil and eternal destiny hangs upon its answer.

4. It is a decisive question. It calls for a definitive answer once and for all. No more delaying, excusing, or halting. Only two sides may be found—that of Satan and the world and that of Christ and the church. No man can plead neutrality. Not to be on one side is to decide for the other.

Spurgeon says, "I feel that he tarries in a position at once hazardous and sublime, for whichever that choice shall be, it means eternity; it means Heaven and all its glories, or it means Hell with all its terrors. Whether the man shall be for God or for his enemies will mean for that man kinship with angels or league with devils. It shall mean for him the white robe and the everlasting song of adoring praise, or it shall mean the blackness of darkness and the perpetual wailing of unending misery."[162]

Which side will be chosen? May you tell the Lord what Amasai said to David, "Thine are we, David, and on thy side, thou son of Jesse."

"Decide not the question on any doubtful or insufficient grounds, lest you deceive your own souls, and perish amidst the enemies of God."[163]—Charles Simeon.

51

Joshua asked: "What mean these stones?"

"What mean these stones?" (Joshua 4:21). There are sermons in stones.

1. Memorial stones, as referenced in the question, testify to the mighty work of God (Joshua 4:19). The pillar of twelve stones, set up in Gilgal, became a memorial to the nation of what Jehovah did for them. The children's question, "What mean ye by these stones?" was answered by reciting the miracle God wrought at Jordan, enabling the ark to pass over on the dry ground (the stones were taken from that dry waterbed).

2. Milestones that marked the distance of two miles to the Jew that carried the backpack of a Roman soldier speak of doing more than the required to help another for the sake of Christ (Matthew 5:41). Christians are to go the second mile with the ungodly, cantankerous and offensive, displaying the love of Christ.

3. Millstones (used for grinding grain and could weigh hundreds of pounds) are forewarned of the judgment that awaits him, which causes a young believer to become disheartened or doubtful in the faith (Luke 17:2).

4. Stumbling stones speak of the influencer of another weaker in the faith to be wounded (discouraged, disappointed) or fall into sin by observing their liberty (Matthew 18:6).

5. Stepping stones symbolize the person who enhances another's spiritual growth, stamina, and success (1 Peter 2:5). Barnabas was a huge stepping stone to Paul (Acts 9:27). Jonathan was such to David (1 Samuel 23:16).

6. The two tablets of stone speak of man's unchanging moral compass and standard (Exodus 24:12). The code of morality by which man is to govern life and relationships (toward God and his fellow man) is the Ten Commandments.

7. Landmark stones define the boundaries of property ownership (Proverbs 22:28), but spiritually, they may apply to Holy Scripture as God's "boundary stone" to govern belief and conduct.

8. Cemetery stones preach loudly of the brevity of life and its conclusion of work and witness, God's judgment, and eternity either in Heaven or Hell (John 11:39). Every cemetery stone has etched upon it the words, "Prepare to meet thy God" (Amos 4:12).

Heed the sermons of the stones—their witness and warning.

"The stones must have tongues in order that their testimony may be more complete."[164]—R. S. MacArthur.

52

The disciples asked: "What shall be the sign of thy coming?"

"What shall be the sign of thy coming and of the end of the world?" (Matthew 24:3 KJ21). Jesus responded to the disciples' question with several indicators of His return. They include false Christs who deceive many (Matthew 24:5), wars between nations (Matthew 24:7), famines and earthquakes (Matthew 24:7), persecution of the saints (Matthew 24:9–10), false prophets (Matthew 24:11), apostasy (Matthew 24:12), and the Gospel's declaration to the entire world (Matthew 24:14).

Jesus further states that His coming will be at a time similar to Noah's. "But as the days of Noah were, so shall also the coming of the Son of man be" (Matthew 24:37). Five characteristics of Noah's day will be manifest when Christ returns.

1. It will be a time of sickening corruption. "The earth was corrupt in God's sight" (Genesis 6:11a NIV). The most shameful acts were committed and permitted in Noah's day (Genesis 6:5). "As the days of Noah were, so shall also the coming of the Son of man be."

2. It will be a time of widespread violence. "The earth…was full of violence" (Genesis 6:11b NIV). The strong terrorized the weak in Noah's day. Today, no more does one war end than another begins. Murders, assaults, kidnappings, and store pillage are becoming more commonplace (2 Timothy 3:1). Terror and fear envelop man's heart. "As the days of Noah were, so shall also the coming of the Son of man be."

3. It will be a time of defiant irreligion. "And spared not the old world, but saved Noah the eighth person, a preacher of righteousness, bringing in the flood upon the world of the ungodly" (2 Peter 2:5). Noah's day was marked by indifference to the spiritual and sacred. Faith was receding. The voices of the spiritual were mocked, disdained, and ignored. The people heeded not the preaching of Noah to repent and return to God. They feared not the judgment of God (Hebrews 10:31). "As the days of Noah were, so shall also the coming of the Son of man be."

4. It will be a time when pleasures dominate man's life. "In the days that were before the flood they were eating and drinking, marrying and giving in marriage" (Matthew 24:38). The materialistic inundated the religious. The people of Noah's day were preoccupied and absorbed with the cares and pleasures of life to the flagrant neglect of the spiritual. "Choked with…pleasures of this life" (Luke 8:14), they were "lovers of pleasures more than lovers of God" (2 Timothy 3:4). "As the days of Noah were, so shall also the coming of the Son of man be."

5. It will be a time of unexpected judgment. "They knew not until the flood came" (Matthew 24:39 ASV). For years, the colossal structure of the Ark stood before them, bearing witness to the coming Judgment, yet they refused to hear or believe its warning and that of Noah. They could have known and should have known of its coming. Instead, they were surprised and unprepared when the judgment arrived (Genesis 7:16). Religious ignorance, insensitivity, and the pursuit of worldly pleasures and possessions bring false security to the soul, resulting in unforeseen and unanticipated judgment. "As the days of Noah were, so shall also the coming of the Son of man be."

Upon witnessing the things that characterized Noah's day, Jesus says, "Then look up, and lift up your heads; for your redemption draweth nigh" (Luke 21:28). Don't simply embrace His coming; expect it and be ready for it (Matthew 24:44). Spurgeon advises, "Oh, Beloved, let us try, every morning, to get up as if that were the morning Christ would come! And when we go to bed at night, may we lie down with this thought, *Perhaps I shall be awakened by the ringing out of the silver trumpets heralding His coming.* What a check, what an incentive, what a bridle, what a spur such thoughts as these would be to us!"[165] Maranatha! Vance Havner says, "I'm not looking for signs. We've had plenty of them. I'm listening for a sound."

"Do not make the blunder of the ship carpenters in Noah's time, who helped to build the ark but did not get into it."[166]—T. De Witt Talmage.

53

Gideon asked: "With what shall I save Israel?"

"And he said unto Him, 'Oh my Lord, with what shall I save Israel? Behold, my family is poor in Manasseh, and I am the least in my father's house.' And the Lord said unto him, 'Surely I will be with thee, and thou shalt smite the Midianites as one man'" (Judges 6:15–16 KJ21). To Gideon's feeling of inadequacy for the task, the Lord offers two words of encouragement. First, God assured him of

His presence in the quest. Second, He assured Gideon of success. He would defeat the Midianites as if they were but a single person. Matthew Henry asserts, "He assures him of success; for *if God be for us, who can* prevail *against us?* If He be with us, nothing can be wanting to us. The presence of God with us is all in all to our prosperity, whatever we do."[167]

But Gideon doubted the promise. "Then Gideon said to God, 'You said that you would help me save the Israelites. Give me proof'" (Judges 6:36 ERV). Hindson says, "His question as to whether or not God would save Israel by his hand implies that he was still afraid to fully trust God's promise."[168] To bolster his faith in what was promised, Gideon asked God to let dew fall on a fleece overnight but keep the ground about it dry. It came to pass as requested. But Gideon still wasn't convinced that God would give him victory over Midan. Therefore, he requests God to keep the fleece dry overnight but cause the ground around it to be wet. Once again, it happened as requested. Criswell, "He was attempting to strengthen his declining faith."[169]

Saith G. A. Rogers, "The only question with this mighty man of valor was, 'Is the Lord indeed with me? Is He on my side? Can I possibly have made any mistake? I do not doubt the Lord's power. If He will, He can save Israel by my hand. I will ask for a sign from the Lord.' He did so, and you know with what result."[170] Note that God did not reprimand Gideon for the fleece test but displayed patience and understanding in giving what his inaptness summoned.[171] "A bruised reed shall he not break, and the smoking flax shall he not quench" (Isaiah 42:3). The two miracles of the fleece and the dew instilled Gideon with the trust and courage necessary to battle Midan victoriously.

Note, don't judge Gideon's cautionary steps too severely. God didn't. It is better to ask for a sign of proof to proceed than to press forward rashly only to be mistaken. F. B. Myer said, "We have no right to ask for signs for the gratification of a morbid curiosity, but we are justified in asking for the concurrence of outward providence indicating the will of God."

"God delights in strengthening fragile faith. Far better to admit weakness and ask for strengthening than to go into battle with a cocky faith."[172]—James E. Smith.

54

David asked: "Is the child dead?"

"Is the child dead? And they said, He is dead. Then David arose from the earth, and washed, and anointed himself, and changed his apparel, and came into the house of the LORD, and worshipped: then he came to his own house; and when he required, they set bread before him, and he did eat" (2 Samuel 12:19–20).

Death, at times, is God's love at work, protecting a child from future hardship, heartache, and hurt. Isaiah says, "The good men perish; the godly die before their time, and no one seems to care or wonder why. No one seems to realize that God is taking them away from evil days ahead. For the godly who die shall rest in peace" (Isaiah 57:1–2 TLB). What a consoling thought!

David's manner of coping with his son's death provides comfort and guidance to parents who experience such horrendous grief (2 Samuel 12:18–24).

1. David was sustained by the belief that his son was saved. In his mind, there was no doubt that his son was with God. Matthew Henry says, "God calls those his children that are born unto Him; and, if they are His, He will save them."[173]

2. David embraced religious hope (2 Samuel 12:23b). He anticipated a reunion with his son. "Let the hope 'full of immortality' be our stay in our dark hour. No 'counterfeit immortality,' but the continuance, in a higher sphere of being, of the conscious, complete, personal existence, now certified by Christ's resurrection. This can give patience in suffering and solace in death."[174] Note, a child in Heaven retains his identity. "Then [in Heaven] shall I know even as also I am known" (1 Corinthians 13:12). Criswell states that one's personality survives in Heaven and

that we will be who we are now without the baggage of sin and imperfection.[175]

3. David leaned heavily upon his future immortality (2 Samuel 12:23). 'I can't bring him back to me, but I can go to him.' The chiefest comfort in the death of a child hinges upon knowing a reunion awaits.

4. David understood that incessant grieving could not bring the child back (2 Samuel 12:22–23). As long as the child was alive, he prayed and fasted in the hope of the child's recovery. David had to reconcile himself to the fact the child was dead and "move on" with life, as difficult as that was. Note that grief that is currently visible will, in time, be borne invisibly.

5. David's grief was enveloped in peace (2 Samuel 12:20). He went into the house of the Lord and worshiped. Peace flows from worship, communion, and praise (Isaiah 26:3). Peace is instilled by focusing on to whom the child has gone and from what they have been taken, not upon the unanswerable why.[176]

"This may comfort us when our children are removed from us by death—they are better provided for, both in work and wealth, than they could have been in this world. We shall be with them shortly, to part no more."[177]—Matthew Henry.

55

Absalom asked: "Is this thy kindness to thy friend?"

"Is this thy kindness to thy friend? Why wentest thou not with thy friend?" (2 Samuel 16:17).

When David left Jerusalem, Absalom immediately seized the city. Absalom asked Hushai, a leading politician of the time and an intimate friend of David, why he didn't remain with David. Hushai replied that it was because of his hearty support of Absalom. In truth, at David's bidding, Hushai returned to Jerusalem, attached himself to Absalom as a spy, and conveyed counsel that favored David. Absalom's sarcastic words, "Is this thy kindness to thy friend?" were true, but not in the way he imagined.

"It's not *what we have* in life, *but who we have* in our life that matters." Solomon said, "Sweet friendships refresh the soul and awaken our hearts with joy, for good friends are like the anointing oil that yields the fragrant incense of God's presence" (Proverbs 27:9 TPT). A good friend, the highest tier kind, will exhibit ten traits or characteristics.

1. A friend supports in difficulty. "A friend loveth at all times, and a brother is born for adversity" (Proverbs 17:17). Friends are sensitive to each other's hurts and needs. They can show up when you need them (phone call, visit, letter, text) and stay the course until the need is met or the trial is over. Ulysses S. Grant said, "The friend in my adversity I shall always cherish most. I can better trust those who helped relieve the gloom of my dark hours than those who are so ready to enjoy the sunshine of my prosperity with me."

A man became lost in the wilderness. Another approached him, and the following conversation ensued: "Sir, I am lost. Can you show me the way out of this wilderness?"

"No," said the stranger, "I cannot show you the way out of the wilderness, but maybe if I walk with you, we can find it together." A friend walks with us through life's sorrows, suffering, and hardships until we find a way out together. Saith Spurgeon, "Many might have failed beneath the bitterness of their trial had they not found a friend."

2. A friend sweetens life. Cicero says, "Friendship improves happiness and abates misery by doubling our joy and dividing our grief." Lawson remarks, "A well-chosen friend sweetens the present life and assists us in our progress to a better self."[178] Someone has said, "A friend lives to make life less difficult for another."

3. A friend keeps secrets. Friends are trustworthy. They never divulge confidences. Bridges said, "Would we have our friend rest his anxieties on our bosom (Proverbs 17:17), let him not see the results of misplaced confidence dropping out of our mouth."[179]

4. A friend won't let go. A friend's love, loyalty, and faithfulness are never failing. Matthew Henry said, "Where God unites hearts,

carnal matters are too weak to separate them."[180] "Friends love through all kinds of weather" (Proverbs 17:17 MSG).

5. A friend has your back. Friends are dependable in every high and every low. Whatever the circumstance, a friend stays the course. "There are 'friends' who pretend to be friends, but there is a friend who sticks closer than a brother" (Proverbs 18:24 TLB).

6. A friend is quick to forgive. Keep a giant cemetery in the backyard to bury the faults of a friend. The closest of friends, at times, disappoints. All have feet of clay. Friends quickly forgive the wounds inflicted by a loving and caring friend.

7. A friend invests in the friendship. The best friendship is the one cultivated to become increasingly better. Over time, strangers may become friends, but friends may become strangers unless the relationship is nourished. Oscar Wilde says, "Ultimately, the bond of all companionship, whether in marriage or friendship, is conversation."

8. A friend's happiness is linked to that of his friend. Aristotle defined friendship as a "single soul, dwelling in two bodies." Keller writes, "Friends voluntarily tie their hearts to one another. They put their happiness into their friends' happiness, so they can't emotionally flourish unless their friends are flourishing too."

9. A friend strengthens your spiritual walk. In a time of grave difficulty for David, Jonathan helped him strengthen his grip on God (1 Samuel 23:16). Strengthening another's grip on God through prayer, encouragement, fellowship, and sharing of biblical insights is essential to friendship.

10. A friend remains near and dear until the end. Helen Keller wrote, "True friends are never apart, maybe in distance but never in heart."

We all need a friend of the highest tier (the David/ Jonathan type) to walk alongside us to make life's journey more endurable, enjoyable, excitable, and profitable. "Two are better than one....For if they fall, the one will lift up his fellow. But woe to him that is alone when he falleth, for he hath not another to help him up" (Ecclesiastes 4:9–10 KJ21). Eleanor Roosevelt said, "Many people will walk in and out of your life, but only true friends will leave footprints in your heart."

"A true friend unbosoms [unloads] freely, advises justly, assists readily, adventures boldly, takes all patiently, defends courageously, and continues a friend unchangeably."—William Penn.

56

Thomas asked: "How can we know the way?"

Regarding His departure to Heaven, Jesus told the disciples not to fear or "let [their] heart be troubled," for He would return for them. In response, Thomas asked, "How can we know the way?" (John 14:5). Jesus answered by saying, "I am the way, the truth, and the life: no man cometh unto the Father, but by me." Note:

1. Christ is the "Way" man is reconciled to God and eternal life. "For there is one God, and one mediator between God and men, the man Christ Jesus" (1 Timothy 2:5). In Christ, the sinner is pardoned of sin and granted access into the presence of God. Christ is not one of many ways to reconciliation with God (salvation), but man's only way. "No one comes to the Father, but by me" (John 14:6 RSV). Tozer says, "Jesus is not one of many ways to approach God, nor is He the best of several ways; He is the *only* way."

2. Christ is the "Truth," the embodiment of all that is true and excellent (John 14:6b). Carson says, "Jesus is the truth because He embodies the supreme revelation of God—He Himself 'narrates' God."[181] As Truth, Christ reveals light to the darkness and depravity in man's soul. He contradicts falsehood and reveals deception. He not only is Truth but possesses truth. "Thy word is truth" (John 17:17). His promises are sure and dependable (Psalm 119:30).

3. Christ is the "Life," the source of abundant and eternal life (John 14:6c; John 10:10). Christ is man's paraclete, constant companion, comforter, and helper, making life meaningful, bearable, and happy. Barclay states, "In the last analysis, what man is always seeking for is life. His search is not for knowledge for its own sake, but what will make life worth living."[182] Christ is "the resurrection

and the life," raising those that die to newness of life (John 11:25) to dwell with Him and loved saved ones eternally in Heaven (John 14:2–3).

Belief in Christ as the Way, the Truth, and the Life prompts submission to and profession of Him as Lord and Savior. Thomas à Kempis asserts, "Without the Way, there is no going; without the Truth, there is no knowing; without the Life, there is no living. 'I am the Way which thou oughtest to follow; the Truth which thou oughtest to trust; the Life which thou oughtest to hope for. I am the inviolable Way, the infallible Truth, the Godliest Life. If you remain in My way, you shall know the truth, and the truth shall free you, and you shall lay hold on eternal life.'"

"Every sinner has a three-fold need—reconciliation, illumination, regeneration. This threefold need is perfectly met by the Savior. He is the Way to the Father; He is the Truth incarnate; He is the Life to all who believe in Him."[183]—A. W. Pink.

57

Paul asked: "And how shall they preach, except they be sent?"

"How then shall they call on him in whom they have not believed? And how shall they believe in him of whom they have not heard? And how shall they hear without a preacher? And how shall they preach, except they be sent?" (Romans 10:14–15). The apostle uses a series of questions to detail the process of salvation.

1. Believing (faith) comes from knowledge (Romans 10:17). MacArthur says, "True faith always has content—the revealed Word of God."[184]

2. Knowledge comes from hearing.

3. Hearing comes from preaching.

4. And preaching comes from God's sending.

Note the sending out of preachers to proclaim the message of Christ's death and resurrection is pivotal to man's salvation. After all, "How shall they hear without a preacher? And how shall they preach, except they be sent?" Note that Matthew Henry asserts, "None are allowed to go for God but those who are sent by Him; He will own none but those whom He appoints (Romans 10:15). It is Christ's work to put men into the ministry (1 Timothy 1:12)."[185]

All who are sent have 'beautiful feet' (Romans 10:15). What makes them so?

1. The magnificence and preciousness of the Gospel they share.

2. The salvation, peace, joy, and eternal life they offer.

3. The likeness of Christ they imitate.

Note, if sent, a man has no option but to go and preach. Spurgeon says, "A man who has really within him the inspiration of the Holy Ghost calling him to preach cannot help it. He must preach. Friends may check him, foes criticize him, despisers sneer at him; the man is indomitable. He must preach if he has the call of Heaven."[186] A sent man is compelled to say, "For necessity is laid upon me; yea, woe is unto me, if I preach not the gospel!" (1 Corinthians 9:16).

"It is a great comfort to those whom God sends that they go for God, and may therefore speak in His name, as having authority, and be assured that He will bear them out."[187]—Matthew Henry.

58

The Daughters of Jerusalem asked: "What is thy beloved more than another beloved?"

"What is thy beloved more than another beloved?" (Song of Solomon 5:9). The question may be asked by unbelievers to believers regarding the one they love, Jesus Christ. What makes Christ's love better than that of others?

1. Christ's love is better because it is everlasting. Solomon says love is "strong as death" (Song of Solomon 8:6). Real love is as strong as death in that it cannot be removed or diminished from him to whom it is attached, even in the direst of difficulty or adversity. It is invincible. This type of love is manifested supremely by Christ,

who loves His own with everlasting love (Jeremiah 31:3). There is no fear of the diminishment or extinguishment of Christ's love, for it is not fueled by man's works and goodness but by the eternal torch of Christ's own nature. The love of Christ for His own will not fail: "Many waters cannot quench love, neither can the floods drown it" (Song of Solomon 8:7). The believer has been 'set as a seal (unbreakable) upon *Christ's* heart' (Song of Solomon 8:6). Christ, as the believer's high priest, has engraved on the breastplate near His heart the names of His own (Exodus 28:12); also, upon the palms of His hands (Isaiah 49:16). Spurgeon states, "Death is but weakness itself when compared with the love of Christ."[188] "Oh, the deep, deep love of Jesus! Vast, unmeasured, boundless, free, rolling as a mighty ocean in its fullness over me" (S. Trevor Francis, 1931).

2. Christ's love is better because of its costly exhibition or expression. Paul said, "God commendeth his love toward us, in that, while we were yet sinners, Christ died for us" (Romans 5:8). Jesus says, "Greater love hath no man than this, that a man lay down his life for his friend" (John 15:13). And that is precisely what Christ did to save us from destruction and Hell. A. W. Pink said, "Christ died not in order to make God love us, but because He *did* love His people. Calvary is the supreme demonstration of Divine love."

3. Christ's love is better because it is flawless. A sinful nature sullies man's love. The love of best friends disappoints. But not Christ's love, for it is untainted with inferior and selfish motives and human weaknesses. Pilate found no fault in Christ. No man can.

4. Christ's love is better because it is free. The Lord says, "I will love them freely" (Hosea 14:4). The love of Christ is worth the whole world to gain, but it is given and acquired freely (Ephesians 2:8–9). The effort to buy it is futile. Saith Isaiah: "Ho, every one that thirsteth, come ye to the waters, and he that hath no money; come ye, buy, and eat; yea, come, buy wine and milk without money and without price" (Isaiah 55:1).

5. Christ's love is better because it is unchanging. John Owen said, "Though we change every day, yet His love does not change. If his love was not unchangeable, we would perish." Saith Spurgeon, "Nothing binds me to my Lord like a strong belief in His changeless

love."[189] Packer wrote, "There are no inconstancies or vicissitudes in the love of the almighty God."

6. Christ's love is better because it is universal. Adrian Rogers asserts, "There's no one He doesn't love—east and west, north and south. A man may go to Hell unsaved, but he'll not go to Hell unloved."[190]

7. Christ's love is better because it is limitless. Rutherford said: "God's love has no brim or bottom." Ryle states, "The love of Christ towards His people is a deep well which has no bottom."

> The love of God is greater far
>   Than tongue or pen can ever tell;
>   It goes beyond the highest star
>   And reaches to the lowest Hell.
>   – Frederick M. Lehman (1917)

"The black background of sin makes the bright line of [God's] love shine out the more clearly."[191]—C. H. Spurgeon.

59

Paul asked: "What is our crown of rejoicing?"

"For what is our hope, or joy, or crown of rejoicing? Are not even ye in the presence of our Lord Jesus Christ at His coming?" (1 Thessalonians 2:19). The Bible reveals five Heavenly crowns the believer may receive. The imperishable or incorruptible crown is for the believer who, like an athlete, disciplines the body into subjection to Christ (1 Corinthians 9:24–25). The Crown of Life is for the persecuted who endure suffering, and perhaps death, for the cause of Christ (Revelation 2:10). The Crown of Righteousness is for those who look for Jesus' second coming (2 Timothy 4:8). The Crown of Glory is for pastors who faithfully proclaim Christ, feed the flock of God, exhibit spiritual oversight for the flock of God, and lead by worthy example (1 Peter 5:4).

Paul, in 1 Thessalonians 2:19, references the fifth crown, the Crown of Rejoicing, which is reserved for those who win souls to Christ. It states or suggests five benefits of those who win souls.

1. They gain a jewel in their crown for each person won to Christ.

2. They will see their converts in Heaven. Paul says, "For what is it we live for, that gives us hope and joy and is our proud reward and crown? It is you! Yes, you will bring us much joy as we stand together before our Lord Jesus Christ when he comes back again" (1 Thessalonians 2:19 TLB). He anticipated seeing his trophies of grace (converts) in Heaven and declared that would be a great delight and joy. If a soul is in Heaven by my efforts, I shall feel like Samuel Rutherford, who said, "My Heaven will be two Heavens in Immanuel's Land."

Who is now alive forever that we will meet again in Heaven because we shared Jesus with them? (Who will be absent for our failure to speak to them about Him?) Matthew Henry says, "Those that turn men to righteousness, turn sinners from the errors of their ways, and help to save their souls from death (James 5:20) will share in the glory of those they have helped to Heaven, which will be a great addition to their own glory."[192]

3. They share in the fruit of the ones won. He that wins another is credited alongside him with the souls he wins. Kimball, the shoe clerk who won Moody, though never leaving Chicago, was credited with Moody for the million souls he brought to Christ worldwide. To our knowledge, Andrew never preached a sermon. Still, by bringing Peter to Jesus, he became, as Robert Sumner says, the spiritual grandfather of the three thousand souls Peter won at Pentecost (John 1:41–42).

4. They know incomparable joy. "Beyond all controversy," Spurgeon said, "it is a joy worth worlds to win souls."[193] Saith Leonard Sanderson, "When one sees another soul come to the Savior, all the bells of his heart begin ringing in a melody similar to that of the day of his own salvation. When he feels the warm handclasp of the one who has just said, 'I do,' it is like an electric

current that connects with Heaven for a time. Joy inexpressible in human language is experienced."[194]

5. They make a difference in another's life. James says, "Let him know, that he which converteth the sinner from the error of his way shall save a soul from death, and shall hide a multitude of sins" (James 5:20). Spurgeon said, "If we had to preach to thousands year after year, and never rescued but one soul, that one soul would be a full reward for all our labor, for a soul is of countless price."

6. They receive a special honor and commendation at the coming of the Lord.

> Perhaps in Heaven, someday, to me
>   Some sainted one shall come and say,
> "All hail, beloved, but for thee
>   My soul to death had fallen a prey."
> And, oh, the rapture of the thought,
> One soul to glory to have brought.
>   – Author unknown.

"Beloved, there are two big days in the life of a believer: the day on which he believes in the Lord and every day after that when he leads someone to faith in Christ."[195]—Watchman Nee.

60

The Psalmist asked: "Wilt thou not revive us again?"

"Wilt thou not revive us again?" (Psalm 85:6). God revived the Israelites by delivering them from Babylonian captivity, where their hearts drooped in such despair that they could not sing the Lord's song. They now plead for a second reviving of more deliverances, encouragement, and consolation.

1. What is revival? Blackaby states, "Revival is a divinely initiated work in which God's people pray, repent of their sin, and return to a holy, Spirit-filled, obedient, love-relationship with God." Finney says, "Revival is the renewal of the first love of Christians."[196]

Havner states, "Revival is simply New Testament Christianity, the saints going back to normal."

2. Why the need for revival? Moral decadence, biblical compromise, disunity, spiritual coldness, and declension all reveal the need for spiritual renewal and refreshing. Stewart asserts, "A church that needs to be revived is a church that is living below the norm of the New Testament pattern....It is a tragic fact that the vast majority of Christians today are living a subnormal Christian life....The church will never become normal until she sees a revival."

3. What are the benefits of revival? Revival points the carnal to a higher spiritual plane and to a return to their "first love" for God. It produces harmony and unity among the brethren. Revival refreshes and energizes the saint. Revival brings the church back to its evangelistic roots. Many churches have lost the "seeking note" in their purpose for existence ["to seek and to save"]. The farmer who builds a barn must not forget why he built it; the same is true for the church. A return to an evangelistic mindset is imperative in preaching, teaching, and worship, and a revival can be the spiritual catalyst for this to happen. Revival brings renewed joy, excitement, and expectation. Revival wins the unsaved. Revival brings glory to God.

4. How is revival obtained? To experience revival necessitates three things (Revelation 2:5).

Remember the spiritual, healthy estate from which you have fallen. "Let's examine and probe our ways, and turn back to the LORD" (Lamentations 3:40 CSB). With desperation, cry out to God with Job, "Oh that I were as in months past" (Job 29:2), and with David, "Revive me according to Your lovingkindness, So that I may keep the testimony of Your mouth" (Psalm 119:88 LSB).

Repent, confess the sins committed, and turn away from them. John wrote, "If we confess our sins, he is faithful and just to forgive us our sins, and to cleanse us from all unrighteousness" (1 John 1:9). And then,

Return, "do the first works." Get back to communion with God, back to the Bible, back to the prayer closet, back to your "first love," back to obedience to God's Word, back to working for God as you formerly did, back to giving, back to witnessing, and back to faithfulness to the church. Revival fire is flamed in the believer's heart individually before spreading to the church body corporately (2 Chronicles 7:14). "O Lord, send a revival, and let it begin in me!"

"Revivals are a part of God's method of accomplishing His purposes."[197]—W. W. Williams.

61

Solomon asked: "Do you see a man who is hasty in his words?"

"Do you see a man who is hasty in his words? There is more hope for a fool than for him" (Proverbs 29:20 ESV). Solomon asserts there is more hope of turning a moronic man into a scholar than there is of teaching one hasty with his words restraint and self-control. Unless the man bridles his tongue, judgment will fall upon him.

1. A person who is "hasty in his words" blurts out insen-sitive and hurtful remarks without forethought or reflection. Spurgeon said, "Tongues are more terrible instruments than can be made with hammers and anvils, and the evil which they inflict cuts deeper and spreads wider."[198]

2. They make rash promises without consideration of their cost or feasibility.

3. They speak at the wrong time and in the wrong place. Solomon says, "A man hath joy by the answer of his mouth: and a word spoken in due season, how good is it!" (Proverbs 15:23).

4. They speak without first listening. Solomon says, "Whoever gives an answer before he listens is stupid and shameful" (Proverbs 18:13 GW).

5. They speak too much. Solomon says, "Too much talk leads to sin. Be sensible and keep your mouth shut" (Proverbs 10:19 NLT). Plato says, "As empty vessels make the loudest sound, so they that have the least wit are the greatest babblers." There is "a time to keep silence, and a time to speak" (Ecclesiastes 3:7). "We have two ears and but one tongue that we may hear much and talk little."

Restrain the tongue from speaking impulsively, inconsiderably, injuriously, and improperly. Say with David, "I will guard my ways, that I may not sin with my tongue; I will guard my mouth with a muzzle" (Psalm 39:1 ESV). Matthew Henry says, "He would keep a muzzle upon it, as upon an unruly dog that is fierce and does mischief; by particular steadfast resolution corruption is restrained from breaking out at the lips, and so is muzzled."

Think before you speak. Weigh your words. Suppress harsh and harmful words. Let God govern the tongue. He who does this will have little to regret or rectify. Note, Christians are concerned about the impact of their words and strive to make every one count for good. Ironside asserts, "The wicked has no such consideration and speaks whatever comes to his lips; let it do what harm it may."[199]

"It is a special mercy to be preserved from hasty judgments, or expression of judgments."[200]—Charles Bridges.

62

David asked: "Put my tears in Your bottle. Are they not in Your book?"

"Put my tears in Your bottle. Are they not in Your book?" (Psalm 56:8 LSB). David asks God to record the tears of his suffering so that He may vindicate him.[201]

God treasures our sundry tears—those shed in times of repentance, those induced by trials, trouble, and sorrow, those caused by spiritual warfare, and those caused over the transgression of evil doers—in His bottle. "What does He keep them [tears] for?" asks Maclaren. "To show how precious they are in His sight and perhaps to suggest that they are preserved for a future use. The tears that His children shed and give to Him to keep…will be given back one day to those who shed them, converted into refreshment, by the same Power which of old turned water into wine."[202]

Not only are our tears kept in His bottle, but His book. What book? The book of His remembrance. Every tear is recorded there. Their number is there; their cause is there; their duration is there; their discomfort is there; their amount is there. Comfort in weeping comes from God noticing all our grievances and grief and observing them with tender, loving concern.[203] As Boice says, "God will never forget nor ever be indifferent to the cares of any one of his much beloved people."[204]

Note, Barnes asserts, "All the tears that we shed are remembered by God. If shed "properly" in sorrow, without murmuring or complaining, they will be remembered for our good; if "improperly" shed—if with the spirit of complaining, and with a want of submission to the divine will—they will be remembered against us."[205]

"In all our wanderings, God watches over us. In all our weaknesses and sorrows, God stands by us with tender compassion for our weaknesses, and with loving consolations for our sorrows."[206]—W. Forsyth.

63

Ethan the Ezrahite asked: "What man is he that liveth, and shall not see death?"

"What man is he that liveth, and shall not see death?" (Psalm 89:48). The Psalm details the promise made to David of the perpetuity of his throne. With calamities and even death threatening the promise's fulfillment, the psalmist pleads for the promise to be soon fulfilled.

Death spares no man. It visits the young and old, the good and the bad alike. Graham said, "All mankind is sitting on death row." Horace said, "The brief sum of life forbids us the hope of enduring long." The Bible says, "It is appointed unto men once to die, but after this the judgment" (Hebrews 9:27). Death is an appointment man will keep on time.

Death often comes by surprise. It surprised Abel in the open field (Genesis 4:8). It surprised King Eglon while sitting in the upstairs room in the palace (Judges 3:21). It surprised Caeser, who was assassinated by a group of senators in the Senate-house at the Curia of Pompey after engaging in 50 battles unharmed.

Death provides no second chances. There are no second chances to be saved beyond the grave. Saith Spurgeon, "What I am when death is held before me, that I must be forever. When my spirit departs, if God finds me hymning His praise, I shall hymn it in Heaven; if He finds me breathing out oaths, I shall follow up those oaths in Hell."

Philip, King of Macedon, had a servant who told him daily, "Remember, sir, that you are a mortal man." Like him, we forget that we face a death day and need reminders of it. Anticipating death is advantageous for six reasons.

1. Coming death prompts diligence in duty. "I must work the works of Him that sent Me while it is day; the night cometh when no man can work" (John 9:4 KJ21). See Ecclesiastes 9:10. Annie Coghill challenges, "Work, for the night is coming; work through the morning hours; work while the dew is sparkling; work mid springing flowers; work when the day grows brighter; work in the glowing sun; work, for the night is coming when man's work is done."

2. Coming death evokes the best use of time. There is no time to trifle (Ephesians 5:16).

3. Coming death motivates our readiness. Isaiah said, "Set thine house in order; for thou shalt die, and not live" (2 Kings 20:1). Amos emphasized the same, "Prepare to meet thy God" (Amos 4:12). How is one to set his house in order for death?

a. The most important thing to do is to become a born-again believer.

b. If estranged from God, square things with Him through confession and repentance (1 John 1:9).

c. Discharge religious duties to God and obligations to man (settle debts, fulfill promises, etc.).

d. Gather essential documents, including funeral plans, life insurance policies, birth certificates, checking/savings accounts, Last Will and Testament, personal loans to others, and usernames/passwords to Internet accounts and store them in a central place known to a family member.

4. Coming death incites holiness. When a Christian believes death is coming, he wants to be as clean (sinless) as possible to face it. Job said, "If I refused to be fair to my slaves when they had a complaint against me, then what will I do when I must face God? What will I say when he asks me to explain what I did?" (Job 31:13–14 ERV).

5. Coming death instills comfort. Spurgeon says, "It is the very joy of this earthly life to think that it will come to an end." Paul states, "For we know that when this earthly tent we live in is taken down (that is when we die and leave this earthly body), we will have a house in heaven, an eternal body made for us by God himself and not by human hands" (2 Corinthians 5:1 NLT).

6. Coming death imparts wisdom. Moses said, "Teach us how short our lives really are so that we may be wise" (Psalm 90:12 ICB). Spurgeon asserts, "To be prepared to die is to be prepared to live." Awareness of death induces salvation through Christ and serious godliness of life.

"It is an excellent art rightly to number our days so as not to be out in our calculation, as he was who counted upon many years to come when, that night, his soul was required of him. We must live under a constant apprehension of the shortness and uncertainty of life and the near approach of death and eternity."[207]—Matthew Henry.

64

**Solomon asked: "Who hath ascended up
into heaven, or descended?"**

"Who hath ascended up into heaven, or descended?" (Proverbs 30:4). The most educated and brightest unbeliever is inapt to answer the question herein posed, "for they are foolishness unto him: neither can he know them, because they are spiritually discerned" (1 Corinthians 2:14). Jesus answered the question in John 3:13: "And no man hath ascended up to heaven, but He that came down from heaven, even the Son of Man which is in heaven." Paul reveals that *Jesus likewise descended:* "Now that He ascended, what is it but that He also descended first into the lower parts of the earth? He that descended is the same also that ascended up far above all heavens, that He might fill all things" (Ephesians 4:9–10).

Christ's descent from Heaven to Earth was redemptive in mission. Peter says, "For Christ also hath once suffered for sins, the just for the unjust, that he might bring us to God, being put to death in the flesh, but quickened [made alive again] by the Spirit" (1 Peter 3:18). Through Jesus' descent to the Cross, He atoned for man's sins and destroyed "him that had the power of death, that is, the devil" (Hebrews 2:14). Three days after being crucified and buried He was raised from the dead. Forty days later, *Jesus ascended* back into heaven. "And when he had spoken these things, while they beheld, he was taken up; and a cloud received him out of their sight" (Acts 1:9).

Paul says, "Wherefore He saith, When He ascended up on high, He led captivity captive, and gave gifts unto men" (Ephesians 4:8). Matthew Henry says, "He conquered those who had conquered us, such as sin, the Devil, and death. Indeed, He triumphed over these on the cross, but the triumph was completed at His ascension, when He became Lord over all, and had the keys of death and Hades put into His hands."[208] Ironside asserts, "The fact of His having gone up and having been received by the Shekinah—the cloud of divine Majesty—testifies to the perfection of His work in putting away forever the believer's sins."[209] MacArthur comments, "The phrase 'when He ascended on high' depicts a triumphant Christ returning from battle on earth back into the glory of the heavenly city with the trophies of His great victory."[210]

Note that Jesus' deity is proclaimed in Proverbs 30:4. He came down to earth to be the mediator between man and God (1 Timothy 2:5). Upon completion of the work (procuring salvation for man through the Cross and resurrection), He ascended back into Heaven (Acts 1:11). The church awaits His glorious descent when she will ascend to Heaven with Him to be forever with Him (John 14:2–3).

"From the hour our Lord left it, this world has lost all charms to us. If He were in it, there were no spot in the universe which would hold us with stronger ties; but since He has gone up, He draws us upward from it. Joseph is no more in Egypt, and it is time for Israel to be gone. No, earth, my treasure is not here with thee, neither shall my heart be detained by thee."[211]—C. H. Spurgeon.

65

King Lemuel's mother asked: "Who can find a virtuous woman?"

"Who can find a virtuous woman?" (Proverbs 31:10). Its answer is, "Almost, no one" because she is an exceedingly precious and rare jewel. Matthew Henry says, "Good women are very scarce, and many that seem to be so do not prove so."[212] Another said, "Nothing so damps the ardor and joy of a man or his children as an incompetent, faulty woman, and nothing can be a greater source of strength than the woman who gives an impulse to all that is good and right and checks the evil by a significant look or a softly spoken word."[213]

Note ten traits of the model woman outlined in the Proverb.

1. Her demeanor. She always presents herself in a dress and person honorably. 'Strength and dignity are in a godly woman's clothing' (Proverbs 31:25).

2. Her disposition. She is cheerful, sweet, kind, and gentle despite the circumstances. 'The law of kindness is on her lips'

(Proverbs 31:26). She bridles her tongue, refusing to gossip and speak harshly.

3. Her counsel. She is a wise counselor. "She openeth her mouth with wisdom" (Proverbs 31:26). Her tongue imparts advice, instruction, and guidance based upon the Holy Scriptures.

4. Her influence.

a. She has an elevating shaping influence in the home.

b. She has an elevating shaping influence on her husband outside the home. "Her husband is known in the gates" (Proverbs 31:23).

5. Her dependability. She stands by her husband in the most trying of times. What a picture of the love of Christ for the church! "A man's greatest treasure is his wife" (Proverbs 18:22 CEV).

6. Her aspiration. She seeks to do only "good" to her husband. "She comforts, encourages, and does him only good and not evil all the days of her life" (Proverbs 31:12 AMP).

7. Her sacred trustfulness. She "laugheth at the time to come" (Proverbs 31:25 ASV). She trusts Jesus with her future (highs and lows) and, therefore, is able to be at rest and peace with whatever happens (Isaiah 26:3).

8. Her devotion.

a. She fears God, absorbs His Word, and walks in righteousness. Methinks, she arises before dawn not only to prepare breakfast for the family but to meet with God and to talk with the servants about Him (Proverbs 31:15). Additionally, she is a prayer warrior for her husband and children. When Dr. Moffat's (missionary to Africa) wife died, his first exclamation on hearing the news was, "For forty-three years, I have had her to pray for me."

b. She displays inviolable faithfulness and devotion to her husband.

9. Her caring. "She stretcheth out her hand to the poor; yea, she reacheth forth her hands to the needy" (Proverbs 31:20). The model woman is compassionate and caring toward others.

10. Her task. "She looketh well to the ways of her household, and eateth not the bread of idleness" (Proverbs 31:27). Her foremost duty, whatever the sacrifice, is to care for the family's needs. Everything else must be secondary. "Home is her sphere, and her work is to make home happy."[214]

The Proverbs 31 woman is prized by her husband and children (Proverbs 31:28). "Her children arise up, and call her blessed [like saying, '*Hooray, hooray for our mother*']; her husband also, and he praiseth her [like saying, 'Best of wives!' 'Noblest of women!']." The results of a godly woman's life are visible. She has a happy husband, appreciative children, a good name, and God's approval.

"Who can find a virtuous woman?" Bridges asserts, "Perhaps one reason of the rarity of the gift is that it is so seldom sought. Too often is the search made for accomplishments, not for virtues; for external and adventitious recommendations, rather than for internal godly worth."[215]

"There is no jewel in the world so valuable as a chaste and virtuous woman."—Miguel de Cervantes.

66

Ezekiel asked: "Should not the shepherds feed the flocks?"

"Should not the shepherds feed the flocks?" (Ezekiel 34:2). Corrupt priests and Levites caused Israel's defection from God and downfall. Ezekiel pronounces God's judgment to them.

When pastors fail to feed the sheep, the sheep are left naked or bare to satanic attack; grow cold, idle, indifferent; and decay spiritually. Solomon says such sheep eventually "perish" for the absence of the Word being preached (Proverbs 29:18). The pastor's task is foremost that of a feeder and nourisher. John Owen said, "The first and principal duty of a pastor is to feed the flock by diligent preaching of the word." And even more emphatically, Owen said, "He is no pastor who doth not feed his flock." Luther said, "A preacher must be both soldier and shepherd. He must nourish, defend, and teach; he must have teeth in his mouth and be able to bite and fight."

What is said on Sunday to be most impactful must "pass through the fire of an intense spiritual life in the preacher."[216] "The fire on the altar must be kept burning; it must never go out." Otherwise, he will preach amidst gray ashes with little power and vitality, and with slumber in the work. May the motto on the preacher's banner and fervent prayer of his heart be that of David Brainerd, "Oh, that I were a flaming fire in the service of my God."[217]

Jesus said of John the Baptist, "he was a burning and a shining light" (John 5:35). "Blessed eulogy! May it be earned by each one of us. 'Burning and shining'—our very ideal of a minister; a hot heart with a clear head; impetuosity and prudence blended; zeal and knowledge linked in holy wedlock."[218] Amen, and amen. Let's keep fanning the flame. New manna is to be gathered "fresh" every morning (Exodus 16:21) to feed the shepherd's soul and prepare him to feed the flock on the Lord's Day.

The good shepherd leads the sheep into "green pastures" to feed on heavenly manna. By the Holy Spirit's power, He makes the feeding refreshing and soul-nourishing. Well-fed sheep respond better to adversity, affliction, sorrow, anxiety, fear, and doubt and are more apt to discharge their Christian duties faithfully.

Spurgeon offers advice as to how to feed the flock. "Give the people every truth baptized in holy fire, and each truth will have its own useful effect upon the mind. But the great truth is the Cross, the truth that 'God so loved the world....' Beloved, keep to that. That is the bell for you to ring. Ring it and keep on ringing it."[219] Frankly, he said, "No Christ in your sermon, sir? Then go home, and never preach again until you have something worth preaching."[220] Amen, and amen.

Remember, pastor, you "must give account" of how you watched over and nourished the souls of the sheep (Hebrews 13:17).

"The hungry sheep look up and are not fed."—John Milton.

67

The Sadducees asked: "In the resurrection, therefore, when they shall rise, whose wife shall she be of them?"

"In the resurrection, therefore, when they shall rise, whose wife shall she be of them?" (Mark 12:23 JUB). Not believing in the resurrection, the Sadducees sought to entangle Jesus with the question (see Mark 12:19–23), showing that belief in the resurrection was absurd. But they failed, for Jesus answered forthrightly, saying, "For when they shall rise from the dead, they neither marry, nor are given in marriage; but are as the angels which are in heaven" (Mark 12:25).

Will we remain united to our spouse in Heaven in a marital role? Will my spouse wait for me, or will they find someone else in Heaven? Jesus teaches believers in Heaven don't stay married to those they married on earth (Luke 20:27–38). But neither will they be married to another. Marriage in Heaven is superseded by something far better—union with Christ (Revelation 19:6–9). Barclay comments, "The risen are like the angels and physical things like marrying and being married no longer enter into the case."[221] Wessel states, "Marriage will not exist as it does now, but all life will be like that of the angels. This means that the basic characteristics of resurrection life will be service for and fellowship with God."[222]

Jesus' words do not mean we will fail to recognize, reunite with, or love our spouse in Heaven. It's the marriage relationship that ceases, not the memory of it. The relationship will change, not the companionship. It will be superior to Earth's by divine design, though this is difficult for the human mind to comprehend.

J. Vernon McGee writes, "This doesn't mean that a man and a woman who were together down here can't be together in Heaven. They [just] won't be together as man and wife… [or] establishing a home up there, nor are they raising children."[223] "As children of God," writes Herschel Hobbs, "we will have a relationship far richer and sweeter than any we knew on earth."[224]

Criswell asserts, "We shall not know less of each other in Heaven; we shall know more. We shall possess our individual names in Heaven. We shall be known as individuals. You will be you; I shall be I; we shall be we. Personality and individuality exist beyond the grave."[225] Love is immortal and eternal.

"There is life after death and therefore a hope of future resurrection. But resurrection is not reconstruction and the continuation of life as it now is. God's children will not become angels, for we shall be like Christ, but we shall be like the angels in that we will not marry or have families. It will be a whole new kind of life."[226]—Warren Wiersbe.

68

The Pharisees asked: "Is it lawful for a man to put away his wife for every cause?"

"Is it lawful for a man to put away his wife for every cause?" (Matthew 19:3). Are there any circumstances in which one can change the "I do?" said in a marriage ceremony to an "I don't" afterward?" Does Scripture sanction any valid grounds for divorce? Jesus grants an exception clause about the no divorce standard in Matthew, saying, "And I say unto you, whosoever shall put away his wife, except it be for fornication, and shall marry another, committeth adultery: and whoso marrieth her which is put away doth commit adultery" (Matthew 19:9).

He states the same exception in Matthew 5:32. This is Jesus's only valid ground for divorce. To divorce and remarry for any other reason is to commit adultery. The word fornication refers to all kinds of gross sexual immorality. This is equally applicable to the wife when divorcing her husband. Criswell elucidates the exception by stating, "Jesus did not teach that the innocent party must divorce the unfaithful one. The purpose of this permission clause is not to encourage divorce for this reason but to forbid it for other reasons. Even when permissible, dissolution is apart from divine intention and ideal. The binding nature of marriage does not depend upon human wills or upon acts of persons but upon the original character of the divinely appointed institution of marriage."[227]

Jesus' teaching on no divorce was so rigid and unbendable that the disciples said following the discourse in Matthew 19, 'It's best not to marry' (Matthew 19:10). Even the "exception" for divorce is to be the absolute last resort. The person who divorces unbiblically may not remarry except to their former spouse (Mark 10:11–12). An unbiblical divorce produces evil consequences (Matthew 19: 9). God doesn't want a person penalized for a divorce, not of their doing, which is evident from Scripture. Therefore, He offers the opportunity for a fresh start in remarriage.

"If you've been divorced, you are not a second-class citizen. There's something called the grace of God. Forgiveness is always available."[228]—Adrian Rogers.

69

James asked: "What causes quarrels, and what causes fights among you?"

"What causes quarrels and what causes fights among you?" (James 4:1 ESV). Who would have thought it? A sharp disagreement ("a heated dispute"[229]) developed between the two premier missionaries of the early church regarding John Mark. Barnabas wanted to take him on the next missionary journey, but Paul didn't (Acts 15:37–41). John Mark's desertion while in the heat of ministry with them in Pamphylia caused Paul's trust to turn to distrust in him (Proverbs 25:19).

Who was right? Insightfully, A. T. Robertson says, "No one can rightly blame Barnabas for giving his cousin John Mark a second chance, nor Paul for fearing to risk him again. One's judgment may go with Paul, but one's heart goes with Barnabas."[230] MacArthur says the weight of evidence favors Paul being right, for Barnabas should have submitted to his apostolic authority in the matter.[231]

Note that Barnabas disappears from the Scriptures and that the Antioch church commended Paul and Silas and not Barnabas and

Mark, which makes it plausible that MacArthur's view is correct. The real question, however, is not "Who was right?" but "Was it right?"

Matthew Henry says, "They were certainly both at fault to be hot as to let the contention be sharp (it is to be feared they gave one another some hard words)."[232] Pollock states, "There must have been serious wrong in the situation which made the loveable, even-tempered Barnabas use angry words, and Paul had far to go before he could write, 'Love is patient and kind....Love does not insist on its own way.'"[233] After the dispute, they depart separate ways, with Barnabas not to be mentioned again outside the reference by Paul to the Corinthians.

What might be learned from Paul and Barnabas' heated dispute?

1. Hot, venomous words imperil relationships. "A few hot words may undo the love of years as a few blows of the axe cuts down the oak of a century's growth."[234] Matthew Henry insightfully states, "Paul and Barnabas, who were not separated by the persecutions of the unbelieving Jews, nor the impositions of the believing Jews, were yet separated by an unhappy disagreement between themselves. Oh, the mischief that even the poor and weak remainders of pride and passion that are found even in good men do in the world, do in the church! No wonder the consequences are so fatal where they reign."[235] Bitter disagreement that leads to heated contention and conflict must always be avoided.

2. Ask the Holy Spirit how you can win without wounding another in times of dispute.

3. Sometimes, taking different roads is necessary. Incompatible differences may necessitate separation. Paul and Barnabas' irreconcilable differences regarding John Mark forced them to separate.

4. Don't allow disagreement to impede ministry. B. H. Carroll said, "Division, even when it springs from quarrels, God can overrule to greater furtherance of the Gospel.[236] The upshot of the sad affair between the two men was that two missionary expeditions resulted (Romans 8:28). The ministry personnel doubled, enabling

the work to be done quicker and more thoroughly. Despite their separation, they both were committed to their intention before the dispute, namely to "visit [their] brethren in every city where [they had] preached the word of the LORD" (Acts 15:32). Barnabas and Mark go to Cyprus (part of the territory where Mark had been faithful on the first tour). Paul and his new associate Silas go to the part of the country that Mark did not visit earlier. Give the men credit for not allowing Satan to use the dispute to stop their ministry.

5. Let a mutual Christian friend mediate or referee sharp disputes to keep them civil and calm. Had these men done this, the story probably would have ended differently.

6. Depart in peace. Paul and Barnabas moved forward peacefully, though separately. Based upon Paul's commendation of Barnabas to the Corinthians, they eventually reconciled (1 Corinthians 9:6) but never reunited.

"The holiest men may have ruffled tempers sometimes."[237]—Joseph Parker.

70

Paul asked: "Know ye not that a little leaven leaveneth the whole lump?"

"Know ye not that a little leaven leaveneth the whole lump?" (1 Corinthians 5:6). Paul reproved the Corinthians for condoning the hideous and reprehensible conduct of one of their members, exhorting them to purge him from the body. The old leaven must be purged out so they can celebrate the Christian Passover properly, a feast that symbolizes their deliverance from the old life in Egypt (Exodus 12:15, 18–19).

With one exception, leaven refers to sin in Scripture (Matthew 13:33). Satan would have man believe that a "little leaven," *one* sin, won't hurt him. But Satan is a liar, and the truth is not in him. It will hurt man and color his life. How powerful is just a "little leaven"?

1. It is malignant. It spreads and corrupts all it possesses. Where leaven is permitted, it will work throughout the whole, regardless of the good flour added.

2. It can alter God's plan.

3. It can spoil the testimony.

4. It can shorten life.

5. It can enslave the soul.

6. It can rob peace.

7. It can diminish spiritual strength.

8. It can corrupt sound doctrine.

9. It robs joy. The saint's song is muzzled in environments not conducive to its spiritual note (Psalm 137:4). "Sin takes all the music out of our hearts."[238]

Don't underestimate the power of "a little leaven." An ocean begins with a drop of water; a stone is a little pebble first, and a rock is a tiny grain. A ruined and devastated life begins with "a little leaven." It's "the little foxes, that spoil the vines" (Song of Solomon 2:15).

Purge the leaven out. Paul says, "Purge out therefore the old leaven, that ye may be a new lump, as ye are unleavened" (1 Corinthians 5:7). Says Spurgeon, "A great sin cannot destroy a Christian, but a little sin can make him miserable. Jesus will not walk with his people unless they drive out every known sin."[239] On certain days, the head of the Jewish household would perform a Jewish ritual. He would search out every particle and crumb of leavened bread in the home and discard it altogether. This was done with the greatest thoroughness, for if only one crumb remained, it could infest the good bread.

The believer must purge every loaf and crumb of leavened bread (sin and its contamination) from the heart with the same diligence and care. None must escape detection, regardless of size, for it will spread its corruption to the rest of the soul.

"To purge out the old leaven, many sweepings of the house will be wanted."[240]—C. H. Spurgeon.

71

The Israelites asked: "What trespass is this that ye have committed against the God of Israel?"

"This is what the whole community of the Lord has said: Why have you committed such an unfaithful act against the God of Israel by turning from the Lord today? When you built an altar for yourselves, you rebelled against the Lord today" (Joshua 22:16 EHV).

A governing rule of life is not to decide a matter until sufficient information is known. "Don't jump to conclusions—there may be a perfectly good explanation for what you just saw" (Proverbs 25:8 MSG). Solomon says, "He that answereth a matter before he heareth it, it is folly and shame unto him" (Proverbs 18:13).

Certain tribes of the Israelites jumped to the wrong conclusion about their brother tribes, Reuben, Gad, and the half-tribe of Manasseh when they built an altar. They wrongly believed it was an act of rebellion and were ready to go to war with them—until they got the whole story (Joshua 22:10–34). Potiphar failed to hear Joseph's side of the story and imprisoned him as a result (Genesis 39:19–20). Christ's case for being the Messiah was determined wrong by the Sanhedrin before it was heard. The same was true for the apostle Paul. Ziba, Mephibosheth's servant, told David that Mephibosheth was in Jerusalem, reclaiming the kingdom of Saul (2 Samuel 16:1–4). David jumped to the wrong conclusion from failure to hear Mephibosheth's side of the story (2 Samuel 19:24–30).[241] When Mephibosheth's side was presented, David learned Ziba had lied.

Hear both sides of a matter without prejudice. Matthew Henry advises, "It is folly for a man to go about to speak to a thing which he does not understand, or to pass sentence upon a matter which he is not truly and fully informed of, and has not patience to make a strict inquiry into; and, if it be folly, it is and will be a shame."[242]

Partial truth or half the story (insufficient information) yields the wrong conclusion.

A man's outward appearance does not necessarily speak to his character and soul condition (John 7:27). Wiersbe asserts, "Too often we are slow to hear—we never really listen to the whole matter patiently—and swift to speak, and this gets us into trouble. A godly person will study to answer, but a fool will open his mouth and pour out foolishness (Proverbs 15:28)."[243] Ironside says, "Rash judgments, founded on one-sided evidence, or formed by jumping at conclusions, expose the unwise one to shame when the case is thoroughly investigated, and he is found to have spoken without proper proof."[244] Get your facts right. Jesus said, "Do not judge according to appearance, but judge with righteous judgment" (John 7:24 LSB).

"Men are often too quick in forming their opinions of other people. A superficial glance is considered enough for an irrevocable verdict. The sentence is pronounced, and the neighbor is characterized before he has had a fair chance of revealing his true nature."[245]—W. F. Adeney.

72

David asked: "What shall be done to the man that killeth this Philistine?"

"What shall be done to the man that killeth this Philistine, and taketh away the reproach from Israel?" (1 Samuel 17:26). David, in his battle with Goliath and subsequent victory, pictures the Lord Jesus Christ.

1. Both were sent by their father.

2. Both were beloved. David's name means "beloved." Jesus is God's beloved Son.

3. Both brought gifts to their brethren.

4. Both were rebuked and rejected by their own. David's brother, Eliab, scolded him. The Jews rejected Christ. "He came

unto his own, and his own received him not." Note, Matthew Henry asserts, "Those that undertake great and public services must not think it strange if they are discountenanced and opposed by those from whom they had reason to expect support and assistance; but must humbly go on with their work, in the face not only of their enemies' threats but of their friends' slights and suspicions."[246]

5. Both answered their critics non-contentiously and kindly. David said "Is there not a cause?" Jesus said, "Wist ye not that I must be about my Father's business?"

6. Both freely battled the enemy.

7. Both refused another's armor. David declined Saul's armor to battle Goliath; Christ declined the sword and shield. They chose to battle in the name of the living God.

8. Both loved the brethren. David and Christ were distraught by the domination of the enemy over the people.

9. Both played the role of meditators. David's battle with Goliath resolved the conflict for the people, and Jesus' battle with Satan on the Cross resolved the conflict for His people (1 Timothy 2:5).

10. Both proclaimed the same motto. "I come to thee in the name of the Lord of hosts."

11. Both were confident. To Saul, David said, "The Lord that delivered me out of the paw of the lion, and out of the paw of the bear, he will deliver me out of the hand of this Philistine" (1 Samuel 17:37). Jesus said, "Destroy this temple, and in three days I will raise it up" (John 2:19). John says, "For this purpose the Son of God was manifested, that He might destroy the works of the devil" (1 John 3:8).

12. Both secured the victory. David cut off Goliath's head with the sword of the giant. Jesus, 'through death, destroyed him that had the power of death, that is, the devil' (Hebrews 2:14). Spurgeon says, "The crucifixion of Jesus, which was supposed to be the victory of Satan, was the consummation of His victory over Satan."[247] Neither stopped battling the enemy until the work was accomplished. On the cross, Jesus said, "It is finished."

13. Both were obedient to their fathers' commands. "David rose up early in the morning, and left the sheep with a keeper, and took, and went, as Jesse had commanded him" (1 Samuel 17:20). Jesus said, "I must work the works of him that sent me, while it is day" (John 9:4).

"The reason some of us are not winning our big battles is because we're losing our little battles."[248]—Adrian Rogers.

73

David asked: "Is there not a cause?"

"Is there not a cause?" (1 Samuel 17:29). Let Eliab protest and deride. Let King Saul question and doubt. Let the army quail in cowardice. David must robe himself in the power of God and battle the giant that dishonors God's name. And he does without hesitation. The question challenges believers to champion a cause for Christ, as he.

1. Identify the cause. "Is there not a cause?" Is there not a sin or evil agenda in high places that compels the Christian to stand and fight for God, like David? Is there a person or people group that needs the message of salvation?

2. Join the cause. Burke said, "All that is necessary for the triumph of evil is that good men do nothing." Note, Jonathan, the mighty warrior, didn't join the cause with David. Christians cannot possibly join every good cause. He must discern which God would have him support.

3. Defend the cause. David non-contentiously replied to his brother Eliab's cruel and vindictive insinuations, saying, "Is there not a cause?" (1 Samuel 17:29). For David, Goliath's dishonor of God was sufficient reason to battle him. Matthew Henry says, "All the world should be made to know that there is a God and that the God of Israel is the only living and true God, and all other pretended deities are vanity and a lie."[249]

4. Win the cause. David saw the cause through to triumph. "David prevailed over the Philistine with a sling and with a stone"

(1 Samuel 17:50). Wiersbe says, "Neither his brothers' criticism nor Saul's unbelief kept David from trusting God for victory."[250] Causes are lost because people fail to stay the course. Persevere in battle until victory is won. In fighting for a good reason, it is always too soon to quit.

"All of us face giants of one kind or another, but we may overcome them through the power of God."[251]—Warren Wiersbe.

74

Isaiah asked: "And he said, "What shall I cry?"

"The voice said, "Cry!" And he said, "What shall I cry?" "All flesh is grass, and all the goodliness thereof is as the flower of the field. The grass withereth, the flower fadeth, because the spirit of the Lord bloweth upon it; surely the people is grass" (Isaiah 40:6–7 KJ21). Isaiah, in hearing a voice, asked, "What shall I cry [proclaim]?" The answer was that all flesh is grass, and the goodness of life is as a flower; they both wither and fade because "the Spirit…bloweth upon it."

The *Spirit of God bloweth* upon man to accomplish His purpose in salvation.

1. The Holy Spirit draws people to Christ. No man can come to Christ unless the Spirit draws him (John 6:44). He is God's agent in regenerating a lost soul.

2. The Holy Spirit convinces man *(bloweth upon him)* of his transgression. "When he [the Holy Spirit] comes, he will prove that the world's people are guilty. He will prove their guilt concerning sin and godliness and judgment" (John 16:8 NIRV). The foundation of the old man (sin and self-righteousness) must be destroyed so that a new and better foundation in Christ can be erected. This is done primarily through the Law (Ten Commandments). Spurgeon states, "The Law is the needle, and you cannot draw the silken thread of the Gospel through a man's heart unless you first send the needle of the Law to make way for it. If men do not understand the Law, they will not feel that they are sinners."[252]

With the aid of the Holy Spirit, the clearer the presentation of the Law, the deeper the penetration of the Law, the greater the destruction and purging of unrighteousness. G. Campbell Morgan said, "The trouble with people who are not seeking a Savior and for salvation is that they do not understand the nature of sin. It is the peculiar function of the Law to bring such an understanding to a man's mind and conscience."[253]

3. This work of the Holy Spirit distresses the soul. Acknowledging sin brings painful guilt and misery until confessed and cleansed by Christ (1 John 1:7). Such pain prompts souls to call in the middle of the night for the preacher to point them to Christ! Joy follows the mourning.

4. The Holy Spirit transforms the soul (1 Corinthians 5:17; Titus 3:5). "Now the mindset of the flesh is death, but the mindset of the Spirit is life and peace" (Romans 8:6 CSB). Jesus calls this work of the Spirit the New Birth (John 3:3).

Note, if the Holy Spirit does not persuade a man to believe because of his transgression of the Law and the Gospel's truthfulness, nothing else can. With this assertion, Spurgeon agrees, saying, "If the voice of God from the top of Sinai and His voice by Moses in the book of the Law, if His voice by the divers [various] prophets in the Old Testament, and especially His own word by His own Son, who hath brought immortality to light by the Gospel, cannot convince men, then there is nothing in the world that can of itself accomplish the work."[254]

"Without the presence of the Spirit, there is no conviction, no regeneration, no sanctification, no cleansing, no acceptable works....Life is in the quickening Spirit."[255]—W. A. Criswell.

75

Judas asked: "Why was not this ointment sold for three hundred pence, and given to the poor?"

"Why was not this ointment sold for three hundred pence, and given to the poor?" (John 12:5).

In Bethany, at the house of Simon the Leper, a woman (we know her to be Mary, the sister of Martha and brother of Lazarus) entered with an alabaster box (vase that held perfume) of ointment (genuine perfume made in India that was highly costly) and poured it upon Jesus' head. John adds, "And wiped his feet with her hair: and the house was filled with the odor of the ointment" (John 12:3 ASV).

Both Christ's head and feet were anointed. An uproar developed from Judas and others who counted the act a waste of "money." They argued that the perfume "might have been sold" for more than a year's wages. As they became vehement toward her, Jesus sternly said to Judas, the ringleader of the verbal attack, "Let her alone" (Mark 14:6). He then vindicated Mary's gracious act of generosity, saying, "She hath wrought a good work [worthy of praise and honor] on me" (Mark 14:6). (That good work was the anointing of His body "aforehand" for burial, the symbol of His forthcoming death). Mary's love and gratitude to Christ will be memorialized wherever the Gospel is preached.

Observations gleaned from the story:

1. Gratitude considers no cost too great to express it. The giver counts a jar of expensive perfume as "the least I can do" in response to its recipient's kindness.

2. Gratitude may be misinterpreted by outsiders. Judas, blinded by the love of money, misunderstood Mary's act. People blinded to gratitude consider a gratuitous gift a ploy to gain love, favor, position, and promotion.

3. Gratitude flows from the heart touched by another's caring action. Mary's expression of gratitude was spontaneous from the heart, prompted by His kindness and goodness toward her.

4. Gratitude is a gift informing its recipient that the kind deed done did not go unnoticed or unappreciated.

5. Gratitude is remembered. Mary's gratuitous act to Jesus was two thousand years ago and is still remembered. Displays of loving and deep gratitude live forever in the heart of its recipient.

"He is ungrateful who denies that he has received a kindness bestowed upon him; he is ungrateful who conceals it; he is ungrateful who makes no return for it; most ungrateful of all is he who forgets it."—Seneca the Younger.

76

The angels asked: "Why stand ye gazing up into heaven?"

"Ye men of Galilee, why stand ye gazing up into heaven? This same Jesus, which is taken up from you into heaven, shall so come in like manner as ye have seen him go into heaven" (Acts 1:11). Matthew Henry paraphrases the question, "Why stand you gazing, as men frightened and perplexed, as men astonished and at their wits' end?"[256] Forty days after the resurrection, the disciples witnessed Jesus' ascension to Heaven. As they gazed upon Him ascending, two angels suddenly appeared and stood beside them. Note two things they did.

1. The angels mildly rebuked the disciples for tarrying after He disappeared from sight ("Why stand ye gazing?"). Why was their gaze prolonged? Possibly for any of six reasons.

a. They watched in case He would reappear.

b. They watched, knowing they would not see Him again for a while.

c. They watched, perhaps to see if there would be commotion in the clouds (Isaiah 24:23).

d. They watched, doubting they would ever see Him again.

e. They watched because they were captivated by the moment's intensity.

f. They watched out of confusion and fear.

Whatever the reason or reasons, the reprimand reminded them of their need to get to work carrying out the Great Commission: 'Go into all the world and preach the Gospel to every creature, beginning at Jerusalem.' Matthew Henry asserts, "When we stand gazing and trifling, the consideration of our Master's second coming should quicken and awaken us; and, when we stand gazing and trembling, the consideration of it should comfort and encourage us."[257]

2. The angels confirmed several facts about Christ's return.

a. Christ will return personally—"this same Jesus." We don't want an amended Christ but the same Christ who walked before man on earth.

b. Christ will return bodily. He left clothed in His resurrected body. He will return clothed with it.

c. Christ will return unexpectedly and suddenly. "While they looked," He went. He will come back in like manner. "Therefore be ye also ready: for in such an hour as ye think not the Son of man cometh" (Matthew 24:44).

d. Christ will return with the clouds. "A cloud received Him out of their sight." The Bible says He will return with the clouds. "Behold, he cometh with clouds" (Revelation 1:7).

e. Christ will return in glory. He departed with glory—His return will be marked with glory.

f. Christ will return from Heaven. He ascended to Heaven. "He was received up into heaven." (The battle was done, the victory was won, and God welcomed His Son home.) He will return from Heaven.

Note, Jesus ascended unassisted. Luke says that "while they worshipped, He was carried up into heaven," and again, "He was received up....He was taken up" (Luke 24:51; Acts 1:2, 9). Chadwick remarked, "Physical interference is not implied: no angels bore Him aloft; and the narratives make it clear that His glorious Body, obedient to its new mysterious nature, arose unaided."[258]

Note, the two angels' promise of Christ's return comforted the disciples, for Luke states that they returned to Jerusalem that same hour with great joy (Luke 24:51–52). "The Heaven that gives back Christ gives back all we have loved and lost, solves all doubts, and ends all sorrows."[259]

[Christ ascended] "to assure the saints of their ascension also; for it is to His God and their God, to His Father and their Father, that He is ascended; and therefore they shall ascend also, and be where He is, and be glorified together with Him; and all this is to draw up their minds to Heaven, to seek things above, where Jesus is; and to set their affections, not on things on earth, but on things in Heaven; and to have their conversation there; and to expect and believe that they shall be with Christ for evermore."[260]—John Gill.

77

The author of Hebrews asked: "Are they not all ministering spirits?"

"Are they not all ministering spirits, sent forth to minister for them who shall be heirs of salvation?" (Hebrews 1:14). Angels are "ministering spirits" to the redeemed. The Greek word for *minister* refers to "serviceable labor and assistance."[261] "They are ministering spirits, or Heavenly assistants, who are continually active today in building the body of Christ—advancing the ministry of Jesus and the building of His church."[262] Their earthly assignment is to benefit the redeemed church of God. McDonald says, "They [angels] serve those who are saved from the penalty and power of sin but not yet saved from the presence of sin; that is, those believers who are still on earth."[263]

They are God's messengers to do as He bids. The psalmist says, "Bless the LORD, ye his angels, that excel in strength, that do his commandments, hearkening unto the voice of his word" (Psalm 103:20). God sent the angel Gabriel to assist Daniel (Daniel 9:21), Zacharias (Luke 1:19) and Mary (Luke 1:26).

Note, angels are not servants *of* the church, but Christ's servants *to* the church.[264] "Praise the Lord, all you warriors [angels] of his, you servants [angels] of his who carry out his desires" (Psalm 103:21 NET). Biblical references to angels ministering to saints include Lot (Genesis 19), Elijah (1 Kings 19:4–8), Elisha (2 Kings 6:16–17), Daniel (Daniel 6:22; 9:20–27; 10:10–21), Zacharias (Luke 1:11–20), Mary (Luke 1:26–38), the shepherds (Luke 2:9–14), Mary Magdalene and other women (Luke 24:4–7; John 20:11–13), the apostles immediately after the ascension (Acts 1:10–11), the apostles in prison (Acts 5:19–20), Peter (Acts 12:7–10), Paul (Acts 27:23–24). Angels ministered to Christ in the wilderness of temptation (Matthew 4:11) and Gethsemane (Luke 22:43).[265]

Angels perform various services on behalf of the Lord to the saint.

1. They escort saints from Earth to Heaven at death. Lazarus, at his death, "was carried by the angels into Abraham's bosom [Heaven]" (Luke 16:22). David Jeremiah says, "For every Christian, the time is coming when we will move into our Heavenly homes, assisted by the Lord's real estate agents—called angels."[266]

2. They protect saints. Their outstanding power and strength ("excel in strength") safeguard the saint against the wiles of the Devil, adversaries, and mishaps. The psalmist declared, "For he will order his angels to protect you wherever you go" (Psalm 91:11 NLT). Spurgeon states, "If our eyes could be opened, we should see horses of fire and chariots of fire about the servants of the Lord; for we have come to an innumerable company of angels, who are all watchers and protectors of the seed royal."[267] Angels are dispatched by God, especially in times of emergency, to warn, help, and protect the saints (Daniel 6:22). "Much of their work is to oppose the malice of evil spirits, who seek our hurt, and to defend us from their rage and subtlety (deceptiveness; skill to be unnoticeable)."[268]

"When struggling against overwhelming difficulties," states F. B. Myer, "when walking the dark, wild mountain pass alone; when in peril or urgent need; we are surrounded by invisible forms, like those which accompanied the path of Jesus. They keep pace with the swiftest trains in which we travel. They smooth away the heaviest difficulties. They garrison with light the darkest sepulchers. They bear us up in their hands, lest we should strike our foot against a stone."[269]

3. They observe saints. Paul says, "We have become a spectacle to the entire world—to people and angels alike" (1 Corinthians 4:9

NLT). Angels can see saints on earth and serve as their encouragers and helpers.

4. They comfort saints. An angel comforted and strengthened Daniel (Daniel 10:19).

5. They show saints how to worship. Angels constantly worship God night and day in an exemplary fashion. "And let all the angels of God worship Him" (Hebrews 1:6).

6. They take their orders from God. Saints, though ministered to by angels, have no authority over them; only God does. Scripture says, "For he will command his angels to protect you in all your ways" (Psalm 91:11 ISV).

"Many an escape from imminent peril, many an unexpected assistance, many a bright and holy thought whispered in the ear, we know not whence or how, is due to those bright and loving spirits."—F. B. Myer.

78

The Eunuch asked: "What doth hinder me to be baptized?"

"What doth hinder me to be baptized?" (Acts 8:36). Upon his salvation, the Eunuch requested to be baptized. Note six things about New Testament baptism.

1. The meaning of it. Baptism pictures and mirrors Jesus' death, burial, and resurrection. It portrays the believer's introduction into His family by death to self, burial to sin, and resurrection to newness of life. "Therefore we are buried with him by baptism into death: that like as Christ was raised up from the dead by the glory of the Father, even so we also should walk in newness of life" (Romans 6:4). In baptism the believer bears witness to his Lord and Savior. "Whosoever therefore shall confess Me before men, him will I confess also before My Father which is in Heaven" (Matthew 10:32).

2. The method of it. "They both went down into the water, both Philip and the eunuch, and he baptized him" (Acts 8:38 KJ21). The word *baptizo* means "to immerse." It never meant "to sprinkle or dip" in New Testament times. Adrian Rogers says, "The method and the meaning are inextricably interwoven; you cannot change the method without destroying the meaning."[270] Mosheim asserts that baptism, in the first century, "was performed by an immersion of the whole body in the baptismal font."[271]

3. The mandate of it. Luke declared, "Repent, and be baptized" (Acts 2:38). Observance of baptism is not a suggestion; it's a command of our Lord to be obeyed by all His followers. Rice says, "God's people should be baptized because God commanded it, not because some church requires it."

4. The model of it. Jesus walked eighty miles to the Jordan River to be baptized by John the Baptist. This He did to announce to the world His redemptive mission through its symbolism (death, burial, and resurrection). As our example, we must follow in His steps in baptism to proclaim the same. Peter said, "Christ also suffered for us, leaving us an example, that ye should follow His steps" (1 Peter 2:21).

5. The misconception of it. Some advocate that baptism is not important. If it wasn't important, Jesus would not have been baptized, commanded His followers to be baptized, and established baptism as an ordinance in the church to be observed until His return (Matthew 28:19–20). J. C. Ryle says, "We ought to regard the sacrament of baptism with reverence. An ordinance of which the Lord Jesus Himself partook is not to be lightly esteemed. An ordinance to which the great Head of the Church submitted ought to be ever honorable in the eyes of professing Christians."

6. The motive of it. Ironside states, "To the lover of the Lord Jesus Christ, there can be nothing legal about baptism. It is simply the glad expression of a grateful heart recognizing its identity with Christ in death, burial, and resurrection. Many of us look back to the moment we were thus baptized, which was one of the most precious experiences we have ever known."

"Here is water"! What doth hinder *you* from being baptized?

"Baptism is an outward expression of an inward faith."—Watchman Nee.

79

David asked: "What is man?"

"What is man?" (Psalm 8:4). Clarke paraphrases the question: "What is wretched, miserable man; man in his fallen state, full of infirmity, ignorance, and sin?" Craigie says the question is asked to evoke the resounding answer, "Nothing!" He explains, "In such vastness, it is inconceivable that human beings have significance or meaning; it is inconceivable that God could remember each human being or give attention to each person."[272] Yet He does. Psalm 8:3–6 stands out in the book of Psalms for it underscores God's love and concern for man despite his despicable condition and rebellious attitude toward Him.

"What is man?" Ask Isaiah, "What is man?" and he answers, he is but "grass" (Isaiah 40:6). Ask Jeremiah, "What is man?" and he answers, man is "deceitful above all things, and desperately wicked" (Jeremiah 17:9). Ask David, "What is man?" and he answers, all classes of men are worthless and deceitful—"a lie" (Psalm 62:9). Ask Job, "What is man?" and he answers, man is a "worm," a mere maggot (Job 25:6). Ask Moses, "What is man?" and he answers, "a living soul" (Genesis 2:7).

Ask Spurgeon, "What is man?" and he answers, "This is an unanswerable question. Infinite condescension can alone account for the Lord stooping to be the friend of man. That He should make man the subject of election, the object of redemption, the child of eternal love, the darling of infallible providence, the next of kin to Deity, is indeed a matter requiring more than the two notes of exclamation found in this verse."[273]

Why is God interested in man who spurns His Word and profanes His name? It is because man is stamped with His divine image, is created with His divine plan, is the object of His divine love, and is the crown of His divine creation (made a little lower than the angels). These reasons, in part, explain why God counts man as the apple of His eye and magnifies him above all creation (Job 7:17) and why He "spared not His own Son, but delivered Him up for us all" to provide salvation from the captivity and penalty of sin. To summarize, Matthew Henry asserts, "Though man is a worm, yet God puts a respect upon him, and shows him an abundance of kindness; man is, above all the creatures in this lower world, the favorite and darling of Providence."[274]

"Oh, the grandeur and littleness, the excellence and the corruption, the majesty and meanness of man!"—Pascal.

80

Peter asked: "Why has Satan filled your heart to lie to the Holy Spirit?"

"But Peter said, 'Ananias, why has Satan filled your heart to lie to the Holy Spirit and to keep back part of the proceeds of the land?'" (Acts 5:3 EHV). Five lessons may be gleaned from the narrative.

1. The wrong motive in giving leads to deceit. Prompted by pride not to be outdone by Barnabas, Ananias and Sapphira lied about the amount of money they had given.

2. Either the heart is filled with the Holy Spirit or Satan.[275] Lies reveal the presence and control of Satan, the father of lies. Lloyd-Jones says of Satan, "His dominant characteristic is that he always produces a lie."[276] Solomon's list of the seven terrible things God hates includes "a lying tongue" (Proverbs 6:17). Note, lying to man is, in reality, lying to God (Act 5:4).

3. Deceitfulness originates in the heart. Peter asked Ananias, "Why hast thou conceived this thing in thine heart?" (Acts 5:4). Solomon states, "Above everything else, guard your heart; for it is the source of life's consequences" (Proverbs 4:23 CJB).

4. Sin concealed will be revealed. "Be sure your sin will find you out" (Numbers 32:23). The Holy Spirit detects the darkest

secrets, bringing them to the light of day (Luke 8:17). Too commonly, men underestimate His presence and power to discover their sins.

5. Accomplices in sin share in its judgment. Sapphira, Ananias' conspirator in the deceitful act, met the same fate as he—immediate death. The judgment saved them from further sin and preserved the church from the spread of hypocrisy. Note, a believer may be removed to Heaven prematurely based on a sin committed and its impact on the kingdom of God (1 John 5:16; 1 Corinthians 11:30).

The bottom-line: God detests hypocrisy (godly pretentiousness) and punishes it (Matthew 23:27). Charnock says, "It is a sad thing to be Christians at a supper, heathens in our shops, and devils in our closets."

"Sin has many tools, but a lie is the handle which fits them all."[277]—Oliver Wendell Holmes.

81

Jeremiah asked: "Why do the wicked prosper?"

"Why do the wicked prosper?" (Jeremiah 12:1 CJB). Jeremiah wrestled with why good things happen to bad people while bad things happen to good people. His problem was that when he compared his well-being and prosperity to that of the ungodly, they prospered and got along better, and he was resentful that God allowed such to happen.

Why do the wicked prosper while the same good is withheld from the righteous?

1. Perhaps God withholds a benefit afforded to the wicked from the righteous because it would prove harmful. "Alteration of circumstances often creates a change of manners."[278]

2. Perhaps God withholds a benefit afforded to the wicked from the righteous because it would interfere with compliance with His plan.

3. Perhaps God withholds a benefit afforded to the wicked from the righteous because it would weaken his dependence upon Him.

4. Perhaps God withholds a benefit afforded to the wicked from the righteous because it would prove hurtful to others.

Why do the wicked prosper better at times than the righteous?

1. Perhaps God prospers the wicked greater than the righteous to benefit others.[279]

2. Perhaps God prospers the wicked greater than the righteous to punish the righteous. "He hath often made wicked men the instruments of His vengeance to bring His people back to their duty and to make them learn righteousness."[280]

3. Perhaps God prospers the wicked greater than the righteous to bring them low suddenly. "They are utterly consumed with terrors." Rawlinson says, "There is something very striking in the suddenness with which the prosperity of a wicked man often collapses. Saul, Jezebel, Athaliah, Epiphanes, and Herod Agrippa are cases in point; likewise, Nero, Galerius, and Julian."[281] "Worldly prosperity," says Horne, "is as the narrow and slippery summit of a mountain, on which, to answer the designs of His providence, God permits the wicked, during His pleasure, to take their station; till, at length, the fatal hour arrives, when, by a stroke unseen, they fall from thence, and are lost in the fathomless ocean of sorrow, torment, and despair."[282]

4. Perhaps God prospers the wicked greater than the righteous to bring them to faith. Paul says, "Don't you realize that God's kindness is supposed to lead you to change your heart and life?" (Romans 2:4 CEB).

The Psalmist, battling the dilemma, escaped his jealousy and envy over the wicked's prosperity and success by entering "into the sanctuary of God" (Psalm 73). There, among the company of God's children, worshipping God and hearing the Word proclaimed, he was convinced that in the end, under God's justness, the righteous would fare better than the wicked.

"If the wicked flourish and thou suffer, be not discouraged; they are fatted for destruction, thou art dieted for health."[283]—Fuller.

82

David asked: "Whom shall I fear?"

"The Lord is my light and my salvation; whom shall I fear?" (Psalm 27:1).

David was no coward but rather one of the boldest men in history. Yet this great warrior, hero of Israel, and mighty man of God states that he had his times when he was afraid. All do. In such times, what are we to do?

1. Embrace God as the Rock of your salvation. Maclaren said, "Only he who can say, 'The Lord is the strength of my life' can say, 'Of whom shall I be afraid?'"[284] Calvin's triple shield of protection against various terrors that threatened was that of David, "My Light, My Salvation and My Defense (or bulwark)."[285] Barnes says, "If God is on our side, or is for us, we can have no apprehension of danger. He is abundantly able to protect us, and we may confidently trust in Him. No one needs any better security against the objects of fear or dread than the conviction that God is his friend."[286]

2. Trust God despite what circumstances seem to say. Fear is often induced by a lie parading as truth. Simpson remarks, "Fear is born of Satan, and if we would only take time to think a moment, we would see that everything Satan says is founded upon a falsehood. When Satan tells you, therefore, that some ill is going to come, you may quietly look in his face and tell him he is a liar. Instead of ill, goodness and mercy shall follow you all the days of your life."[287]

3. Rest in the assurance of God's love. The Bible states, "Where God's love is, there is no fear, because God's perfect love drives out fear" (1 John 4:18 NCV). Fear has no place in love. "We cannot fear if we understand God's love toward us."[288] Adrian

Rogers says, "When you see God's mighty power on one hand and His mighty love on the other, fear melts away. Rest in that love. Say, 'Lord, no matter what happens to me, I know You love me.'"[289] Gurnall says, "The chains of love are stronger than the chains of fear."[290]

4. Rely on God's promise not to abandon. The Bible states in Hebrews 13:5, "He hath said, I will never leave thee, nor forsake thee." The presence of Jesus aboard the "ship" calms and rests its passengers when all around it is tumultuous. Fear is conquered and replaced with calm and peace when the heart says, "Yea, though I walk through the valley of the shadow of death, I will fear no evil: for thou art with me; thy rod and thy staff they comfort me" (Psalm 23:4). Trust is not a feeling that all will work out for the best; it is an abiding conviction based upon God's Word that it will (Romans 8:28).

5. Tap God's power. G. Campbell Morgan says, "The man who measures things by the circumstances of the hour is filled with fear; the man who sees Jehovah enthroned and governing has no panic."[291] Piper asserts, "The presence of hope in the invincible sovereignty of God drives out fear."[292]

"The powers of darkness are not to be feared, for the Lord, our light, destroys them; and the damnation of Hell is not to be dreaded by us, for the Lord is our salvation."[293]—C. H. Spurgeon.

83

David asked: "Wilt not thou deliver my feet from falling?"

"Wilt not thou deliver my feet from falling, that I may walk before God in the light of the living?" (Psalm 56:13). David probably wrote this when his life was in danger at the hands of the Philistines. In confident hope of deliverance, he prays for rescue. The word "falling" may be applied to any false step we make in the Christian life.[294] The text corresponds to the New Testament, Jude 24.

The risk of falling looms great.

1. From doctrinal error. Spurgeon said, "False doctrine is a deadly poison that must be identified, labeled, and avoided."

2. From sin. Demas' love for the pleasures of the world caused his spiritual relapse. More than one mighty man of God has been cut down by sin. Sin, not necessarily sins, can undo the Christian walk in a moment.

3. From devotion. Neglect of a quiet time suffocates the flame in the soul.

4. From liberalism. Compromise and conformity to an adulterated belief system devastate the vine.

5. From duty. Temptations to quit one's post abound among pastors and people alike. Says Spurgeon, "The only course open to us is to plow right on to the end of the furrow and never think of leaving the field till the Master shall call us home."[295]

6. From false teachers. "Hold fast the form of sound words" (2 Timothy 1:13). Don't sit "in the seat of the scornful" (Psalm 1:1).

7. From doubt. Elizabeth Elliot says, "Don't dig up in doubt what you planted in faith." But that's precisely what Satan seeks to get the believer to do.

No fleshly restraint secures us from falling. "The arm of flesh will fail you; you dare not trust your own." No ten-step program guide secures us from falling. No preacher secures us from falling. None but Christ can keep the believer from falling.

Jude said, "Now unto Him that is able to keep you from falling, and to present you faultless before the presence of His glory with exceeding joy" (Jude 24). Christ is the believer's protector, defender, deliverer, guardian, and preserver. Says Spurgeon, "None can deliver us from former guilt or keep us from daily faultiness in the future but the Savior Himself."[392]

"Though Christians be not kept altogether from falling—yet they are kept from falling altogether."—William Secker.

84

Solomon asked: "Who is able to stand before envy?"

"Who is able to stand before envy?" (Proverbs 27:4). "Envy is rebellion," states Erwin Lutzer, "against God's leading in the lives of His children. It's saying that God has no right to bless someone else more than you."[296] Stalker says, "What! Do we grudge that humanity should be served and God glorified by powers superior to our own?"[297]

Envy is an ugly-spirited attitude and action toward others. Abel's murder by Cain, Joseph's bitter treatment by his brothers, David's forced exile by Saul, Daniel's night in the lion's den, and Jesus' arrest and trial all were precipitated by the rottenness of envy. Envy prompts people to do the most vicious, malicious, and meanest things imaginable to make themselves appear better than others (Romans 1:29).

Is hidden in your heart a spirit of envy about the success or prosperity of another, a disposition to speak of their faults and failings rather than their gifts and virtues that excel that of yourself?

Moody shared the fable of an eagle envious of another that could fly better and higher. The eagle approached an archer and said, "I wish you would bring down that eagle up there." The archer replied he would if provided some feathers for his arrow. The envious eagle pulled one out of its wing. The arrow was shot, but it fell short of the rival eagle. The first eagle pulled out another feather, then another, until so many were gone that it couldn't fly. The archer killed the helpless bird. Moody's application: if you are envious of others, the one you will hurt the most by your actions is yourself.

Robert Ann states, "Our safety, our only safety, lies in the renewal and sanctification of our nature by the Holy Ghost."[298]

"The envious man is impoverished by another man's riches and tormented by another man's happiness."[299]—George Lawson.

85

Solomon asked: "Can a man take fire in his bosom, and his clothes not be burned?"

"Can a man take fire in his bosom, and his clothes not be burned?" (Proverbs 6:27). The son replies to the father's question, saying, "Of course not." The same answer must be echoed when the question is applied to adultery to which the text refers.

There are eight good reasons not to play with sexual temptation.

1. Playing with sexual temptation puts the soul directly on immorality's disastrous path. Paul exhorts, 'Give no place to the devil' (Ephesians 4:27).

2. Playing with sexual temptation weakens the resistance to it over time. Ironside asserts, "How many a dreadful blot upon an otherwise upright and honored life has resulted from what at first was a thoughtless familiarity, which led on step by step to the awful overthrow of uprightness and virtue, culminating in life-long sorrow."[300]

3. Playing with sexual temptation works against the Holy Spirit's effort to keep you from it. The command is to "flee…youthful lusts," "abstain from fornication," and "do not commit adultery." To violate the command is to quench the power of the Holy Spirit. To yield to the Spirit's place and power in the temptation grants deliverance. "As you yield to the dynamic life and power of the Holy Spirit, you will abandon the cravings of your self-life" (Galatians 5:16 TPT).

4. Playing with sexual temptation brings the soul into affinity with it.

5. Playing with sexual temptation positions a person for defeat, not victory. The apostle Paul states, 'Do not sow unto the flesh' (Galatians 6:8). To sow to the flesh is to stroke it mentally or physically instead of renouncing and crucifying it. A person sows to the flesh by planting its sensual seeds in the mind. So many fall into sexual sin because they sow to the flesh, positioning themselves for defeat.

6. Playing with sexual temptation is to strike matches to wood without the expectation of kindling a fire.

7. Playing with sexual temptation softens the heart toward the act.

8. Playing with sexual temptation inevitably leads to the act that, in turn, brings havoc and heartache.

"The best and surest defense against promiscuity," says Criswell, "is tender and loving affection between husband and wife."[301] Solomon says, "Let her be as the loving hind and pleasant roe; let her breasts satisfy thee at all times; and be thou ravished always with her love" (Proverbs 5:19).

"Few that are entangled in the sin of adultery recover from the snare."—Thomas Watson.

86

Solomon asked: "Who can say, I have made my heart clean, I am pure from my sin?"

"Who can say, I have made my heart clean, I am pure from my sin?" (Proverbs 20:9). The rhetorical question implies the answer, "Nobody."

We must acknowledge that sin is a fact—that no one is free from it.

1. Everyone is guilty of the defilement of original sin. Paul states, "When Adam sinned, sin entered the entire human race. His sin spread death throughout all the world, so everything began to grow old and die, for all sinned" (Romans 5:12 TLB). David testified, "Behold, I was shapen in iniquity; and in sin did my mother conceive me" (Psalm 51:5). All people are guilty of inherent sin from Adam and Eve. Thomas Brooks says, "There is the seed of all sins—of the vilest and worst of sins—in the best of men."

2. Everyone is guilty of sin by choice. Solomon says, "There is no man that sinneth not" (1 Kings 8:46). Paul attests, "All have sinned" (Romans 3:23). John said, "If we say that we have no sin,

we deceive ourselves, and the truth is not in us" and "If we say that we have not sinned, we make Him a liar, and His Word is not in us" (1 John 1:8, 10). None are innocent of breaking the Law (Ten Commandments) at one point or another. Denied sin is sin still. Bridges says, "A sinner in his self-delusion may conceive himself to be a saint."[302]

3. No one can attain sinless perfection, but all should press toward it. Only one "knew no sin," and that was Christ.

4. Everyone needs to acknowledge and repent of their sins. David cried out to God, saying, "I acknowledge my transgressions: and my sin is ever before me" (Psalm 51:3). Ironside says, "When all pretense to purity in oneself is given up, it is found in Christ, for those who receive Him."[303] John states, "If we confess our sins [agree with God about them, pleading for forgiveness], He is faithful and just to forgive us our sins, and to cleanse us from all unrighteousness" (1 John 1:9). "Print every word of that in diamonds," said Spurgeon about Jeremiah 31:34: "I will forgive their iniquity, and I will remember their sin no more."[304]

"Though we can say, through grace, 'We are cleaner than we have been,' yet we cannot say, 'We are clean and pure from all remainders of sin.'"[305]—Matthew Henry.

87

Isaiah asked: "Who hath believed our report?"

"But they have not all obeyed the Gospel. For Isaiah saith, 'Lord, who hath believed our report?'" (Romans 10:16 KJ21). The rhetorical question referenced Isaiah's message of redemption to Israel. Many were disobedient to it (Isaiah 53:6). Futuristically, it also referenced the negative response to the gospel message acclaiming Christ as the Messiah, which is sent or broadcast to the world. The prophecy was fulfilled: Jesus "came unto His own (the Jews), and His own received Him not" (John 1:11). Isaiah pictures Christ as the Messiah in Isaiah 53.

Despite widespread disobedience (unbelief) to the gospel message, its declaration must not be discouraged or deterred. Ezekiel avidly said, "And they, whether they will hear, or whether they will forbear, (for they are a rebellious house,) yet shall know that there hath been a prophet among them" (Ezekiel 2:5). Why should man believe our report?

1. It is an authoritative report. God authorized believers to proclaim it to all people (Acts 1:8; Matthew 28:18–19).

2. It is a revelatory report. "That which had not been told us, we see." The Gospel is good news, informing man of what was unknown.

a. That God has provided a redeemer to save His people from their sin.

b. That forgiveness of sin and rightness with God and escape from condemnation in Hell is possible.

c. That salvation is attainable by repentance of sin and faith in Christ.

3. It is a trustworthy report. Paul said, "Here is a true statement that should be accepted without question: Christ Jesus came into the world to save sinners, and I am the worst of them" (1 Timothy 1:15 ERV). It is an infallible report (Acts 1:3) sent from Him who cannot lie (1 Thessalonians 2:13). The prophets, apostles, and all the redeemed acclaim the report's truthfulness from knowledge and experience.

4. It is a commanded report. Repentance and faith are expected responses to the gospel message. The Bible says, "The times of this ignorance God overlooked, but now He commandeth all men everywhere to repent" (Acts 17:30 KJ21). God has commanded every person to repent and come to Him in faith. Disobedience is punished with a condemnation to Hell (Mark 16:16).

Why doesn't man believe our report?

1. It's due to lack of information. Ignorance of the gospel message impedes its belief. "So then faith cometh by hearing, and hearing by the word of God" (Romans 10:17).

2. It's due to misinformation. Distorted truth about Christ keeps people from the faith (Matthew 24:11). The real Christ must be displayed before the world (John 12:32).

3. It's due to a low appraisal of Christ.

4. It's due to close-mindedness to it. Presumptuous conceit toward the Gospel keeps man from inquiring into its validity.

5. It is due to a deceptive feeling of sufficiency. They count themselves as sufficient apart from Christ. Paul says, "Not that we are sufficient of ourselves to think any thing as of ourselves; but our sufficiency is of God" (2 Corinthians 3:5).

6. It is due to doubt. Doubts and questions about Christ and the Bible hold some back. These, however, could be resolved if probed to their very depth. God promises to give the necessary light to clarify man's religious questions and difficulties if sought honestly and earnestly (John 7:17).

7. It is due to blindness. A man blinded by Satan perceives not the danger of his soul and need for the salvation Christ affords (2 Corinthians 4:4).

"Salvation comes when the message of the Gospel is preached, believed, and then confessed by men. That message must come from the Word of God."[306]—E. E. Hindson.

88

A scribe asked: "Which is the first commandment of all?"

"And one of the scribes came, and having heard them reasoning together, and perceiving that He had answered them well, asked Him, 'Which is the first commandment [not first in order, but weightiness] of all?' And Jesus answered him, 'The first of all the commandments is: "Hear, O Israel, the Lord our God is one Lord. And thou shalt love the Lord thy God with all thy heart, and with all thy soul, and with all thy mind, and with all thy strength;" this is the first commandment'" (Mark 12:28–30 KJ21).

What kind of love is it that Christ commands of His followers?

It is a preferred love for Christ that stands above all others.

It is a pleasurable love that finds bliss abiding in Christ's presence.

It is a pleasing love that longs to delight Christ.

It is a persistent love that is undisturbed.

It is a proving love demonstrated by obedience to His commandments and submission to His will.

It is a privileged love made possible by Christ's love for us.

John says, "So you see, our love for him comes as a result of his loving us first" (1 John 4:19 TLB). It is a pretentiousless love for Christ, free from hypocrisy, that is dynamic, sincere, and earnest.

Matthew Henry summarizes, "Loving God with all our heart will effectually take us off from, and arm us against, all those things that are rivals with Him for the throne in our souls, and will engage us to everything by which He may be honored, and with which He will be pleased; and no commandment will be grievous where this principle commands, and has the ascendant."[307]

"No other love can be allowed to rival love for God."[308]— William MacDonald.

89

Paul asked: "What fellowship hath righteousness with unrighteousness?"

"Be ye not unequally yoked together with unbelievers: for what fellowship hath righteousness with unrighteousness? and what communion hath light with darkness?" (2 Corinthians 6:14).

A yoke is a wooden bar that couples two oxen to each other and to a pulling beam so they can plow or pull a wagon. An "unequally yoked" team consists of two different sorts of oxen (e.g., a strong ox joined to a weak ox). Instead of completing the task, unequally yoked oxen would go around in circles. One can but imagine the frustration that arose between such a team.

The biblical truth is clear. Christians are not to be united (coupled, yoked) with unbelievers, for the two have different natures, masters, values, world views, and purposes that would cause inevitable conflict and compromise (John 17:16). With this, Matthew Henry agrees, saying, "It is wrong for good people to join in affinity with the wicked and profane; these will draw different ways, and that will be galling and grievous."[309] J. R. Thomson asserts, "No alliance with wicked men can serve any holy purpose."[310]

Consider seven warnings about corrupt, unholy alliances.

1. Confederacy with the ungodly is alignment with the enemy of God. All who are alienated from God are His enemies (Colossians 1:21). James says, "Whoever chooses to be the world's friend makes himself God's enemy!" (James 4:4 CJB).

2. Confederacy with the ungodly makes the fine gold dim (Lamentations 4:1). Tozer said, "One compromise here, another there, and soon enough, the so-called Christian and the man in the world look the same." Adrian Rogers asserts, "It is better to be divided by truth than to be united in error."[311]

3. Confederacy with the ungodly brings defilement and ruin. Solomon said, "The companion of fools shall be destroyed." Matthew Henry asserts, "He that joins in with the evildoers and is aiding and abetting in their evil deeds shall be reckoned, and shall be reckoned with, as one of them."[312]

4. Confederacy with the ungodly impacts the future generations. King Jehoshaphat, a godly king in Judah, made an ungodly alliance with the wicked king Ahab of Israel and even consented to his son's marriage to Ahab and Jezebel's daughter. The first unholy alliance was divinely remedied, but not the second (2 Chronicles 19:1–9). Jehoram, his son, "And he walked in the way of the kings of Israel, like as did the house of Ahab: for he had the daughter of Ahab to wife: and he wrought that which was evil in the eyes of the LORD" (2 Chronicles 21:6).

Upon Jehoram's death, which no one mourned, his wife and son continued to practice the evil he had done (2 Chronicles 22). Even if we recover from an unholy alliance with our faith intact, like

Jehoshaphat, its wanton influence may well bring harm to our children and their children as it did to his son and grandson.

5. Confederacy with the ungodly in one area fosters sympathy and agreement in others.

6. Confederacy with the ungodly hurts the church. If a single beam in the church on Sunday morning gave way, causing the roof's collapse, the whole church would be affected by the single beam. Believers are linked together as living stones in the body of Christ. A believer cannot link or yoke with an unbeliever in his unrighteousness without negatively impacting the entire family of Christ.[313]

7. Confederacy with the ungodly impairs testimony. It hampers the saints' testimony outside and, perhaps even worse, inside the alliance. Sometimes, it's not what we do but our alliance with what others do that spoils the testimony. To ally with the ungodly is to be identified with them and as them. Will Rogers said, "It takes a lifetime to build a good reputation, but you can lose it in a minute."

To encapsulate the teaching of Jesus, shun confederacy with any person or organization whose ideology is contrary to that taught in the Bible. Stay away from all compromising, defiling, and detrimental relationships and enterprises. Barnes says, "There should be a separation. There can be nothing in common between holiness and sin [light and darkness], and Christians should have nothing to do 'with the unfruitful works of darkness.'" "A spiritual relation with the unspiritual is impossible."[314]

> Separate from all that grieves Thee,
>   Separate from sinners, too;
> Yet, like Thee, for sinners caring,
> And, like Thee, with sinners bearing,
>   Asking, "What would Jesus do?"
>   – Lucy A. Bennett (1850–1927)

The command does not mean believers are not to associate to some degree with unbelievers; that would prevent their evangelization, which is the believer's duty (Acts 1:8; Matthew 28:19).[315] Jesus sat with sinners at meat (Matthew 9:10). He was the friend of sinners (Matthew 11:19; Luke 7:34). He developed relationships with sinners, like with the woman at the well (John 4:7). He didn't retreat from the world as a monk, but ministered to people, keeping Himself free from their defilement (John 17:14–15) all to save them.

To the believer unequally yoked with the ungodly, Paul says, "come out from among them, and be ye separate, saith the Lord" (2 Corinthians 6:17). Violating the mandate is to court disaster.

"We are to have no compromising connection with anything in the world which is alien to God."[316]—J. Denney.

90

Micah asked: "What doth the Lord require of thee?"

"What doth the Lord require of thee, but to do justly, and to love mercy, and to walk humbly with thy God?" (Micah 6:8).

What does God want of you? Micah sums it up in three things.

1. To do justly. Outwardly, the believer is to act righteously, honestly, and honorably toward others. Simeon says it is to practice "Truth in our words, and integrity in our actions."[317]

2. To love mercy. Inwardly, the believer is delighted to be compassionate, kind, gentle, and forgiving to those who stumble.

3. To walk humbly. Upwardly, the believer is to walk with God obediently and without arrogance. To obey the requirement, a person must be saved. Living by this moral code is impossible without the power of the Holy Spirit, who indwells the believer.

"Without love, holiness of heart, and righteousness of life, flowing from faith in Christ, all our church-goings, forms of prayer, and almsgivings profit us nothing."[318]—A. R. Fausset.

91

Paul asked: "If the foot shall say, Because I am not the hand, I am not of the body; is it therefore not of the body?"

"If the foot shall say, Because I am not the hand, I am not of the body; is it therefore not of the body?" (1 Corinthians 12:15). The rhetorical answer is a loud, No. The degree and dimension of giftedness do not impact a believer's relationship to the body (Christ). The body of Christ needs many parts—many gifts—to function, as does the physical body. Body parts don't battle for one another's jobs. They cooperate with the other members for the good of the body.

Can you imagine the outcome in the body if the liver insisted on being the kidneys, or the gall bladder, the lungs? To fulfill its purpose on earth, the church, the body of Christ, must exhibit unison and harmony among its many members in the use of their spiritual gift or gifts (Ephesians 4:16). No member of the body of Christ is to feel inferior to the other parts or be treated as inferior by the different parts.

Paul says, "Christ has given each of us special abilities—whatever he wants us to have out of his rich storehouse of gifts" (Ephesians 4:7 TLB).

1. Whatever the gift, don't belittle it.

2. Whatever the gift, don't complain about it. "Does the potter not have the right over the clay, to make from the same lump [of clay] one object for honorable use [something beautiful or distinctive] and another for common use [something ordinary or menial]?" (Romans 9:21 AMP).

3. Whatever the gift, don't squander it. Not to use a gift is a rebuff to God's will and plan.

4. Whatever the gift, don't flaunt it. "Pride goeth before destruction, and an haughty spirit before a fall" (Proverbs 16:18).

"**Whenever a sinner trusts Christ, he or she is made a part of that same body by the operation of the Holy Spirit. The Spirit places** each believer in the body as He sees fit, but each part of the body has an important ministry to perform."[319]—Warren Wiersbe.

92

Paul asked: "Do I seek to please men?"

"For do I now persuade men, or God? or do I seek to please men? for if I yet pleased men, I should not be the servant of Christ" (Galatians 1:10). The charge by the Judaizers that Paul had vacillated in the faith was preposterous. Unlike him, some preachers are guilty of the accusation.

Men-pleasing preaching caters to people's preferences and prejudices at the sacrifice of truth. Sadly, "men would rather be cozened with a pleasing lie than saved with a frowning and threatening truth."[320] Paul says, "For there is going to come a time when people won't listen to the truth but will go around looking for teachers who will tell them just what they want to hear. They won't listen to what the Bible says but will blithely follow their own misguided ideas" (2 Timothy 4:3–4 TLB). Spurgeon said, "A time will come when instead of shepherds feeding the sheep, the church will have clowns entertaining the goats."[321]

Men-pleasing preaching does four things to accommodate the hearer's comfort and satisfaction.

1. It waters down the doctrines. Salvation without the blood, forgiveness without repentance, Heaven without Hell, religion without Christ, and discipleship without sacrifice are preached.

2. It tones down the commandments. The Ten Commandments are preached as the Ten Suggestions, if at all.

3. It brings down the standard. Right and wrong are perverted and altered to appease the conscience. Isaiah said, "Woe unto them that call evil good, and good evil; that put darkness for light, and light for darkness; that put bitter for sweet, and sweet for bitter!" (Isaiah 5:20). The preacher who establishes or approves an unscriptural standard of conduct to gain the approval of man or position will be judged severely.

4. It calms down the guilt. Preaching that arouses guilt is replaced with that which makes the hearers feel good about themselves. It whitewashes man's badness (Proverbs 17:15). Farrer said, "The very guiltiest of sinners [preachers] is he who paints the gates of Hell with the colors of Paradise and gives names of clear disparagement and dislike to scrupulous honor and stainless purity."[322] Note, Solomon says, "He that saith unto the wicked, Thou art righteous; him shall the people curse, nations shall abhor him" (Proverbs 24:24). "For a spiritual ruler [or preacher] to say to the wicked—Thou art righteous," says Charles Bridges, "is indeed perfidious dealing with his Divine Master; cruel deceit to immortal souls; hiding the ruin which he is bound to reveal; acting the part of a minister of Satan, under cover of a minister of Christ. His people will live to curse and abhor him, perhaps throughout eternity."[323]

5. It whittles down the message. It is restrictive preaching confined to several subjects to avoid offense to congregants. Spurgeon cautioned preachers to "beware of picking and choosing in reference to the commands of Christ."[324] To preach the Gospel is to preach its every part. To withhold a single truth of its teaching is to "take away" from its teaching (Revelation 22:19). Preacher, can you truthfully say as Job, "I have not concealed the Words of the Holy One" (Job 6:10)?

Paul indicates that grave punishment awaits those who preach for man's approval (1 Corinthians 9:16). MacArthur says, "God's severest chastening is reserved for unfaithful ministers."[325]

"We must not comply with the wishes or solicitations of men, merely to please them, or to avoid exciting their displeasure."[326]— Charles Simeon.

93

David asked: "Why standest Thou afar off, O Lord?"

"Why standest Thou afar off, O LORD?" (Psalm 10:1). David complains about the wicked and their conduct and questions the delay of God in judging them. The believer in the valley of trouble and suffering often asks the following question.

How might the felt distance between God and us at times be explained?

1. Through understanding that it is not God who moves from us but us from Him by sin. The story of the prodigal son unfolds this truth (Luke 15:11–22).

a. The prodigal left the father, not the father, him. Sin only makes it seem that the reverse is true.

b. The prodigal found the father where he left Him (Hebrews 13:5; 1 Samuel 12:22; Psalm 37:28). Paul said, "If we are disloyal, he stays faithful" (2 Timothy 2:13 CEB).

c. The prodigal found the father joyous, not angry with him. The father runs to him, hugs him, and throws a party for him, reversing what sin had caused him to think would happen. We stand aloof from God by believing He is angry with us over our sins and then complain that He stands far from us when that is not true.

2. Through understanding that God sometimes withdraws His sweet fellowship from the believer or the conscious sense of His presence and power for unknown purposes for our best.[327]

"The presence of God is the joy of His people, but any suspicion of His absence is distracting beyond measure. Let us, then, remember that the refiner is never far from the mouth of the furnace when his gold is in the fire, and the Son of God is always walking in the midst of the flames when His holy children are cast into them."[328]—C. H. Spurgeon.

94

The four lepers asked: "Why sit we here until we die?"

"Why sit we here until we die?" (2 Kings 7:3). The walled city of Samaria lay under siege, and its inhabitants were starving due to a lack of food. Outside the city, the enemy heard the noise of many armies (the noise of Heaven) preparing an attack against them and, in panic, fled, leaving all their food and possessions. Four lepers discovered the deserted camp and plundered it. Thinking of the starving people within the city, they said, "We do not well: this day is a day of good tidings, and we hold our peace" (2 Kings 7: 9). They share the good news of their find with the king, saving the people from starvation.

I know no clearer picture of the believer's responsibility to the unsaved than that of the Four Lepers. Those who have found Christ must tell perishing sinners where He may be found. Note four things about the leper's announcement.[329]

1. They acted without cowardice. Without fear of reprisal from the gatekeeper or king, they told of their find.

2. They acted in union. They collaborated on the story, giving it credence and validity.

3. They acted speedily. Knowing lives were at stake, they proclaimed the news without delay.

4. They acted convincingly—enough, at least, to warrant an investigation into what they said.

Note the progression of their witness. They told the porter or guard at the gate (1 Kings 7:10). The one porter told other porters (1 Kings 7:11a). Those porters told the king's house (1 Kings 7:11b). The king told the people (1 Kings 7:12).

It only takes a spark to get a fire going. The leper's condition prevented them personally from telling all within the city of their find. They told who they could and counted on him to tell the others. And he did. At times, we have to do the same.

As the four lepers, we must not remain silent on this day of Good News!

"The lepers moved from giving up and giving in to giving out. Sharing the good news helped to save the city. We are living in a day of good news. Are you sharing it? We are here not to give in or give up but to give out."[330]—Warren Wiersbe.

95

Job asked: "And where is now my hope?"

"And where is now my hope?" (Job 17:15). Job tells us, "But as for me, I know that my Redeemer lives, and he will stand upon the earth at last" (Job 19:25 NLT).

Unlike secular hope, Biblical hope means certainty, confidence, and assurance of something happening. It's not wishful thinking but undoubtable reality. What is the believer's hope?

1. It consists of the resurrection of the body. Paul said, "If in this life only we have hope in Christ, we are of all men most miserable" (1 Corinthians 15:19). Jesus is proof and the preview of the resurrection. He rose bodily and was recognizable, just as will be the case with every believer (Luke 24:39). Paul says, "Just as we have borne the image of the man of dust, we shall also bear the image of the man of heaven" (1 Corinthians 15:49 ESV). Jesus promises the resurrection in John 11:25: "I am the resurrection and the life. He who believes in Me, though he may die, he shall live" (NKJV).

2. It consists of future life in Heaven. Billy Graham says, "Because Heaven is real, we have hope—hope for the future and hope for our lives right now. No matter what happens to us now, we know it won't last forever, and ahead of us is the joy of Heaven." In Heaven, there will be the absence of sickness, sorrow, and suffering that bring tears to our eyes and hearts (Revelation 21:4).

3. It consists of Christ's return. Paul writes, "Looking for that blessed hope, and the glorious appearing of the great God and our Savior Jesus Christ" (Titus 2:13). Fear, anxiety, despair, and misery are dispelled in the hope of Christ's soon return. Confidence in the hope of His return is undergirded by the fact that He initially appeared as promised by Old Testament prophets and His promise to return in John 14:3.

4. It consists of reunion with loved ones beyond this life. The Bible says, "Then we which are alive and remain shall be caught up together with them in the clouds, to meet the Lord in the air: and so shall *we* ever be with the Lord" (1 Thessalonians 4:17). A

grand reunion day of unending fellowship with loved ones and saints awaits the redeemed at death or the Lord's coming. To know that we will see loved ones and friends again beyond the veil of this life grants unspeakable peace and calm amid grave sorrow. What a glorious Hope we have in Christ Jesus!

"All earthly hopes are, in their very nature, inadequate to our exigencies."[331]—*The Evangelist.*

96

Ahab asked: "Art thou he that troubleth Israel?"

"Art thou he that troubleth Israel?" (1 Kings 18:17). Wrongly, Ahab accused Elijah of being the cause of Israel's trouble (the drought and consequent famine), when *he* was (1 Kings 21:20).

Rutherford states, "Those under the influence of "Ahab's Spirit" are completely blind to the solemn and dangerous reality of their own personal violations of the divine law for which things' sake cometh the wrath of God. They utterly fail to recognize any relation between their thorny and miserable path and the anger of the holy One of Israel, and so must charge those who have opposed their wicked conduct with being responsible."[332]

Many echo Ahab's charge toward preachers and people of God. The ungodly see them as troublemakers, instigators, or agitators. They are viewed as those who 'turn the world upside down' (Acts 17:6) and "do exceedingly trouble our city" (Acts 16:20). When there is a great disturbance in the land, the wicked always spin it to the blame of believers. Spurgeon asserts, "There are many who dare not smite with the hand, who are very busy in laying on their tongue, and this not by exposing our errors, which they have a perfect right to do, but in many cases, the children of God are misrepresented, slandered, abused, persecuted, ridiculed for truth's sake."[333]

Adrian Rogers says of the Ahabs of our day (the corrupt), "They hate God. They hate the church. They hate Christ. They hate the Bible. And they see us as troublemakers; they see us as thorns in their flesh. There are people in America who wish that those of us who name the name of Jesus would get out of their way. The pornographers, the whiskey dealers, the abortionists, and all who have sold themselves to do evil—they hate what we are about."[334]

Note, as a light that shines in the darkness, the believer will always be counted as one "that troubleth Israel." Sin, when exposed, brings discomfort and judgment (Jeremiah 30:15).

"A believer ought to walk through this world expecting to meet with an enemy behind every hedge, reckoning it a wonder if he shall escape for a single day without a bullet from the foe."[335]— C. H. Spurgeon.

97

Moses asked: "Shall your brethren go to war, and shall ye sit here?"

"Shall your brethren go to war, and shall ye sit here?" (Numbers 32:6). The tribes of Gad and Reuben asked to settle in a place already conquered that was ideal for their cattle and livestock. Moses granted the request conditioned on their agreement to join the other tribes in the conquest of Canaan. However, when it came time to battle for Canaan with the other tribes, Moses feared they would refuse to participate.

Moses argued the case for Gad and Reuben's participation in the battle in four ways.

1. They had agreed to it. Failure to join the battle would mean they had lied when they said they would. Not to do what is pledged to a church or a ministry is to have told a bare-faced lie.

2. It was only fair and right for Reuben and Gad to assist the other tribes who helped them conquer the land they possessed to conquer Caanan for their possession. Gratitude, at the least, for the assistance of others in our battles ought to prompt our support of them in their battles.

3. Not joining the battle would discourage and dissuade others from participating. Fewer fighting men could mean the difference

between victory and defeat. Says Spurgeon, "Depend upon it, if we are not serving the Lord our God, we are committing the sin of discouraging our fellow men. They are more likely to imitate our lethargy [and neglect] than our energy."[336] Guard against being a stumbling block to others.

4. Not battling with their brethren would be a sin against the Lord. Moses said to Gad and Reuben, "But if ye will not do so, behold, ye have sinned against the Lord: and be sure your sin will find you out" (Numbers 32:23). Failure to unite with the other tribes in battle would be a sin not only against them but also against God. 'Be sure your sin of idleness, neglect, and loafing in Christian service will find you out,' bringing severe consequences (Numbers 32:8–14).

It is delusive to think this sin will not find you out. Matthew Henry asserts, "Sin will, without doubt, find out the sinner sooner or later. It concerns us, therefore, to find our sins out, that we may repent of them and forsake them, lest our sins find us out to our ruin and confusion."[337]

Moses' reasoning persuaded the two tribes to assist their brethren in conquering Canaan.

"When material gain, not the glory of God, governs our decisions, we will make the wrong decisions."[338]—Warren Wiersbe.

98

Jeremiah asked: "What will you do when the end comes?"

"What will you do when the end comes?" (Jeremiah 5:31 AMP). False prophets and liberal preachers may say what is desired and pleasing, and man may live in disobedience to God, but in the end, what will they do at the Judgment?

"What will you do when the end comes?"

1. It is an unasked question. Not only does a person fail to ask it of himself, but others also fail to ask it of him.

2. It is an unwanted question. People want to forget about the end until the end comes. They shrink away from it, for it forces them to consider the consequences of their unbelief, wanton lifestyle, and judgment before God.

3. It is an unanswerable question. When the end comes, all who are without a wedding garment (salvation) will be "speechless" (Matthew 22:11–12), having no excuse for their unbelief and sin, and be 'cast into outer darkness: there shall be weeping and gnashing of teeth' (Matthew 22:13).

"What will you do in the end?" What will come for you after the end? Isn't it best to consider the question while there is time to modify its answer? Trusting Christ as Lord and Savior avoids a damnable end and eternity. All who repent and trust Christ may honestly answer the question of Jeremiah: "As for me, I will behold thy face in righteousness: I shall be satisfied, when I awake, with thy likeness" (Psalm 17:15).

"An end will come; the end of a wicked life will come when it will be all called over again, and without a doubt will be bitterness in the latter end."[339]—Matthew Henry.

99

Paul asked: "What? know ye not that your body is the temple of the Holy Ghost?"

"What? know ye not that your body is the temple of the Holy Ghost which is in you, which ye have of God?" (1 Corinthians 6:19). The Christian who understands that his body is the dwelling place of Almighty God orders his life accordingly.

1. He dresses appropriately. Matthew Henry observes, "The purity of the heart will show itself in the modesty of the dress."[340] "Blessed are the pure in heart, for they shall see God" (Matthew 5:8 KJ21).

2. He behaves rightly. He abstains from dishonoring conduct that mars the Lord's name. He walks in holiness (Psalm 141:4).

3. He speaks properly. Solomon says, "The mouth of a righteous man is a well of life" (Proverbs 10:11). James said, "Blessing and cursing come out of the same mouth. My brothers, these things should not be this way" (James 3:10 EHV).

4. He thinks guardedly. Paul says, "Think as Christ Jesus thought" (Philippians 2:5 NLV). The believer, mindful that he is the holy temple of God, brings every thought captive to obey Christ (2 Corinthians 10:5).

5. He watches protectively. All forms of impurity and corruption are challenged and resisted (Psalm 101:3).

"The temple of the Holy Ghost must be kept holy. Our bodies must be kept as his whose they are, and fit for his use and residence."[341]—Matthew Henry.

100

Paul asked: "How are the dead raised up? And with what body do they come?"

"How are the dead raised up? And with what body do they come?" (1 Corinthians 15:35).

The saint's spirit immediately enters the presence of the Lord at death; later, at the church's rapture, it will be reunited with its body, which will be transformed into a glorified body likened to that of Christ (1 Thessalonians 4:16; 1 John 3:2; 1 Corinthians 15:53).

"How are the dead raised up? And with what body do they come?" The answer to the first question is that it happens by the omnipotent power of God. The answer to the second question is that its form and substance will be different from that known now. Paul emphasizes the fact, saying, "That which thou sowest, thou sowest *not that body that shall be*" (1 Corinthians 15:37).

In the resurrection, God gives the old body "a beautiful new body—just the kind he wants it to have" (1 Corinthians 15:38 TLB). The resurrected body is superior to the fleshly body in several ways.

1. It will be an imperishable body, unlike the fleshly body, which withers, decays, and dies. It will know no deterioration. "When this perishable will have put on the imperishable, and this mortal will have put on immortality, then will come about the saying that is written, 'Death is swallowed up in victory'" (1 Corinthians 15:54 NASB1995).

2. It will be a glorious body, unlike the fleshly body that bears the marks, consequences, and stigma of sin. Due to the fall in the Garden, we dishonor God by misusing our bodies which were meant to honor and glorify Him completely. Our new body will be an honorable body that is pleasing and honoring to Him.

3. It will be a heavenly body, unlike the fleshly body, with limitations, frailties, and weaknesses. Clarke says it will be "no more liable to weakness through labor; decay by age; wasting by disease; and dissolution by death."[342] Isaiah says, "None there [in Heaven] will say, 'I am sick'" (Isaiah 33:24 CSB). John says, "The former things are passed away" (Revelation 21:4). The psalmist said, "Though ye have lien among the pots, yet shall ye be as the wings of a dove covered with silver, and her feathers with yellow gold" (Psalm 68:13).

4. It will be a spiritual body, unlike the natural, fleshly body, which is fitted only for this world. It must be laid down to gain a spiritual body suited for heavenly living in the world to come. Courson elucidates, "Our present bodies of flesh and blood cannot move into the Kingdom because they're not designed for Heaven. That is what death is all about. For the believer, death is simply a way of leaving our earthly tabernacles and moving into our new bodies, exchanging our crusty brown bulbs for creations of beauty."[343]

5. It will be a powerful body, unlike the fleshly, weak, and impotent body. The extent of its power is not disclosed but will exceed what we possess now.

Note, Jesus' resurrection body is the prototype for the redeemed of God (1 Corinthians 15:20, 48–49; Philippians 3:21; 1 John 3:2). In the resurrection body, He walked, talked, ate, and was recognized

(John 21:1–14). Jesus even dismissed the idea that saints in the afterlife would be "disembodied spirits" (Luke 24:37–39). It was "touchable," therefore "feelable" (John 20:27). Wiersbe states, "It was the same body, yet it was also a different body. The resurrection body retains the personal identity and individuality of the believer, but it will be suited to a new way of life."[344] We will not lose our distinctions as men and women.[345]

"The holy blessed God shall make the bodies of the righteous as beautiful as the body of Adam was when he entered into paradise."[346]—Pinchas.

Endnotes

[1] Needham, George C. *The Life and Labors of Charles H. Spurgeon.* (Boston: D. L. Guernsey, 1887), 7.

[2] Spurgeon, C. H. "Is Anything Too Hard for the Lord?" sermon delivered April 22, 1888, Metropolitan Tabernacle.

[3] Hancock, J. L. *All the Questions in the Bible* (1st ed.). (Logos Research Systems, Inc., 1998).

[4] Spurgeon, C. H. "Strengthening Medicine for God's Servants." Sermon delivered 1875, Metropolitan Tabernacle.

[5] Spurgeon, C. H. "Esther's Exaltation; or, Who Knoweth?" Sermon delivered April 27, 1884, Metropolitan Tabernacle.

[6] Gill, John. *Gill's Exposition of the Entire Bible,* Psalm 119:11.

[7] Spurgeon, C. H. *The Treasury of David: Psalms 111–119* (Vol. 5). (Marshall Brothers, n.d.), 157.

[8] Henry, M. *Matthew Henry's Commentary on the Whole Bible: Complete and Unabridged in One Volume.* (Peabody: Hendrickson, 1994), 914.

[9] Phipps Eyre, C. J. cited in *The Biblical Illustrator,* Psalm 119:11 ("God's Word in the Heart").

[10] Barnes, Albert. *Barnes Notes on the Bible,* Psalm 119:11.

[11] Spence-Jones, H. D. M. (Ed.). *The Pulpit Commentary: Jeremiah,* Vol. 1. (London; New York: Funk & Wagnalls Company, 1909), 217.

[12] Clarke, Adam. *Commentary on the Bible.* (1831), Romans 3:4.

[13] Spence-Jones, H. D. M. (Ed.). *The Pulpit Commentary: Galatians.* (London; New York: Funk & Wagnalls Company, 1909), 277.

[14] Barnes, Albert. *Barnes Notes on the Bible,* Galatians 5:13.

[15] Spence-Jones, H. D. M. (Ed.). *The Pulpit Commentary: Galatians.* (London; New York: Funk & Wagnalls Company, 1909), 271.

[16] MacArthur, J., Jr. (Ed.). *The MacArthur Study Bible* (electronic ed.). (Nashville, TN: Word Pub., 1997), 1798.

[17] MacDonald, W. *Believer's Bible Commentary: Old and New Testaments.* (A. Farstad, Ed.) (Nashville: Thomas Nelson, 1995), 1893.

[18] Henry, M., and T. Scott. *Matthew Henry's Concise Commentary.* (Oak Harbor, WA: Logos Research Systems, 1997), Gal. 5:13.

[19] McGee, J. V. *Thru the Bible Commentary: The Epistles (Galatians)* (electronic ed., Vol. 46). (Nashville: Thomas Nelson, 1991), 95.

[20] MacArthur, John. *Alone with God.* (Colorado Springs, Co: David C. Cook, 2011), 182.

[21] Spurgeon, C. H. "Love at Its Utmost." Sermon delivered September 11, 1887, Metropolitan Tabernacle.

[22] Gill, John. *Gill's Exposition of the Entire Bible,* 2 Corinthians 13:5.

[23] Thiselton, A. C. *The First Epistle to the Corinthians: A Commentary on the Greek Text*. (W. B. Eerdmans, 2000), 1222.
[24] Pratt, R. L., Jr. *I & II Corinthians* (Vol. 7). (Broadman & Holman Publishers, 2000), 262.
[25] Barclay, W., ed. The Letters to the Corinthians. (The Westminster John Knox Press, 1975), 149.
[26] Partially gleaned from Henry, M. *Matthew Henry's Commentary on the Whole Bible: Complete and Unabridged in One Volume*. (Peabody: Hendrickson, 1994), 2417.
[27] Barnes, Albert. *Barnes Notes on the Bible,* James 4:14.
[28] Ibid.
[29] Ibid., Psalm 90:10.
[30] Bradbury, 82.
[31] Henry, M. *Matthew Henry's Commentary on the Whole Bible: Complete and Unabridged in One Volume*. (Peabody: Hendrickson, 1994), 876.
[32] Spurgeon, C. H. "The Happy Christian." Sermon delivered in 1867, Metropolitan Tabernacle.
[33] Orton, J., cited in J. S. Exell. *Proverbs*. (New York; Chicago; Toronto: Fleming H. Revell Company, n.d.), 632.
[34] Exell, J. S. *The Biblical Illustrator: The Psalms* (Vol. 2). (Fleming H. Revell Company; Francis Griffiths, 1909), 355.
[35] Spurgeon, C. H. *The Treasury of David: Psalms 27–57* (Vol. 2). (Marshall Brothers, n.d.), 272
[36] Boice, J. M. *Psalms 42–106: An Expositional Commentary*. (Grand Rapids, MI: Baker Books, 2005), 370.
[37] Ibid.
[38] Dickson, D. *A Brief Explication of the Psalms* (Vol. 1). (John Dow; Waugh and Innes; R. Ogle; James Darling; Richard Baynes, 1834), 237.
[39] Ibid.
[40] Spurgeon, C. H. *The Treasury of David: Psalms 27–57* (Vol. 2). (Marshall Brothers, n.d.), 272.
[41] Craigie, P. C. *Psalms 1–50* (Vol. 19). (Dallas: Word, Incorporated, 1998), 108.
[42] Henry, M. *Matthew Henry's Commentary on the Whole Bible: Complete and Unabridged in One Volume*. (Peabody: Hendrickson, 1994), 754.
[43] Gill, John. *Gill's Exposition of the Entire Bible,* Psalm 144:3.
[44] Barnes, Albert. *Barnes Notes on the Bible,* Psalm 144:3
[45] Spurgeon, C. H. *The Treasury of David: Psalms 120–150* (Vol. 6). (Marshall Brothers, n.d.), Psalm 144:3.
[46] Harman, A. *Psalms: A Mentor Commentary* (Vols. 1–2). (Mentor, 2011), 133.
[47] Hastings, James. *Great Texts on the Bible,* 232.
[48] Joseph Hall, D.D., Bishop of Norwich, 1574–1656.

Endnotes

[49] Henry, M. *Matthew Henry's Commentary on the Whole Bible: Complete and Unabridged in One Volume.* (Peabody: Hendrickson, 1994), 754.

[50] Spurgeon, C. H. "Questions Which Ought to be Asked" (Sermon). https://answersingenesis.org/education/spurgeon-sermons/1511-questions-which-ought-to-be-asked/. Accessed September 28, 2021.

[51] Spurgeon, C. H. "The Eye and the Light." Sermon delivered October 13, 1889, Metropolitan Tabernacle.

[52] Lewis, C. S. *Mere Christianity:* "The Great Sin," Chapter 8.

[53] Exell, J. S. *The Biblical Illustrator: Job.* (Fleming H. Revell Company; Francis Griffiths, 1909), 557.

[54] Ibid., 556.

[55] Hastings, James. *The Great Texts of the Bible: Job to Psalm XXIII,* 121.

[56] Spurgeon, C. H. *Morning and Evening.* (London: Passmore & Alabaster), October 19 (Evening).

[57] Spurgeon, C. H. *Metropolitan Tabernacle Pulpit,* Volume 44. "Songs in the Night," (sermon). Intended for Reading February 27, 1898.

[58] Henry, M. *Matthew Henry's Commentary on the Whole Bible: Complete and Unabridged in One Volume.* (Peabody: Hendrickson, 1994), 726.

[59] Spence-Jones, H. D. M. (Ed.). *The Pulpit Commentary: Job.* (London; New York: Funk & Wagnalls Company, 1909), 574.

[60] Barnes. Commentary on the Bible, Job 35:10.

[61] Spurgeon, C. H. *The Treasury of David: Psalms 56–87* (Vol. 3). (Marshall Brothers, n.d.), 335.

[62] Spurgeon, C. H. *The Treasury of David: Psalms 120–150* (Vol. 6). (Marshall Brothers, n.d.), 227.

[63] Exell, J. S. *The Biblical Illustrator: The Psalms* (Vol. 5). (Fleming H. Revell Company; Francis Griffiths, 1909), 284

[64] Exell, J. S. *The Biblical Illustrator: Proverbs.* (Fleming H. Revell Company), 576.

[65] Ironside, H. A. *Notes on the Book of Proverbs.* (Neptune, NJ: Loizeaux Bros, 1908), 259–260.

[66] Rogers, Adrian. "The Battle of the Bottle" (sermon).

[67] Henry, M. *Matthew Henry's Commentary on the Whole Bible: Complete and Unabridged in One Volume.* (Peabody: Hendrickson, 1994), 2270.

[68] Ryle, J. C. *Christian Leaders of The 18th Century.* (Banner of Truth, Edition 25).

[69] Exell, J. S. *The Biblical Illustrator: Job.* (Fleming H. Revell Company; Francis Griffiths, 1909), 313.

[70] Ibid., 314.

[71] Henry, M. *Matthew Henry's Commentary on the Whole Bible: Complete and Unabridged in One Volume.* (Peabody: Hendrickson, 1994), 1858.

[72] Spurgeon, C. H. "The Good Samaritan." Sermon delivered June 17, 1877, Metropolitan Tabernacle.

Endnotes

[73] Henry, M. *Matthew Henry's Commentary on the Whole Bible: Complete and Unabridged in One Volume.* (Peabody: Hendrickson, 1994), 1858.

[74] Courson, J. *Jon Courson's Application Commentary.* (Thomas Nelson, 2003), 263.

[75] MacArthur, J. *Mark 9–16.* (Moody Publishers, 2015), 81.

[76] Spurgeon, C. H. "Swimming Iron and Sinking Peter," *The Sword and the Trowel,* March 1866.

[77] *The Open Bible: New King James Version* (electronic ed.). (Thomas Nelson Publishers, 1998), Ps 11:4.

[78] McGee, J. V. *Thru the Bible Commentary* (electronic ed., Vol. 2). (Nashville: Thomas Nelson, 1991), 687.

[79] Lawson, G. *Exposition of the Book of Proverbs* (Vol. 1). (David Brown; W. Oliphant; F. Pillans; M. Ogle; Ogle, Duncan, and Co.; J. Nisbet, 1821), 444.

[80] Adams, Jay. *From Forgiven to Forgiving.* (Amityville, NY: Calvary, 1994), 25.

[81] Spurgeon, C. H. *The Treasury of David: Psalms 120–150* (Vol. 6). (Marshall Brothers, n.d.), 415.

[82] Lowery, D. K. In J. F. Walvoord & R. B. Zuck (Eds.), *The Bible Knowledge Commentary: An Exposition of the Scriptures, 1 Corinthians,* Vol. 2. (Wheaton, IL: Victor Books, 1985), 525.

[83] https://www.preceptaustin.org/1_corinthians_927_commentary, accessed November 4, 2022.

[84] Exell, J. S. *The Biblical Illustrator: I Corinthians,* (Vol. 1). (New York: Anson D. F. Randolph & Company), 274.

[85] Spurgeon, C. H. "The Heavenly Race." Sermon Delivered June 11, 1858, New Park Street Chapel.

[86] Wiersbe, Warren W. and David W. Wiersbe. *10 Power Principles for Christian Service.* (Grand Rapids: Baker Books, 2010), 86.

[87] Lewis, C. S. cited in "Hell—Tough Questions Answered." toughquestionsanswered.wordpress.com/category/hell/, accessed April 6, 2011.

[88] Exell, J. S. *The Biblical Illustrator: The Minor Prophets* (Vol. 3). (Fleming H. Revell Company; Francis Griffiths, 1909), 25.

[89] http://christian-quotes.ochristian.com/Backsliding-Quotes/, accessed August 11, 2017.

[90] Exell, J. S. *The Biblical Illustrator: The Minor Prophets* (Vol. 3). (Fleming H. Revell Company; Francis Griffiths, 1909), 27.

[91] Henry, M. *Matthew Henry's Commentary on the Whole Bible: Complete and Unabridged in One Volume.* (Peabody: Hendrickson, 1994), 688.

[92] Ibid.

[93] Wiersbe, W. W. (1996). Be Patient (p. 61). Victor Books.

[94] Henry, M. *Matthew Henry's Commentary on the Whole Bible: Complete and Unabridged in One Volume.* (Peabody: Hendrickson, 1994), 799.

Endnotes

[95] Spurgeon, C. H. *Morning and Evening,* September 2.

[96] Spurgeon, C. H. "The Ethiopian." Sermon delivered May 15, 1884, Metropolitan Tabernacle.

[97] Scarborough, L. R. *With Christ After the Lost.* (Nashville: Broadman Press, 1952), 225-227.

[98] This point adapted from George W. Truett in *A Quest for Souls.* (New York: Harper & Brothers, 1917), 308–309.

[99] Rogers, Adrian. "The Perils of Postponement," Proverbs 27:1. https://www.lwf.org/sermons/audio/the-perils-of-postponement-1051, accessed June 28, 2024.

[100] Spurgeon, C. H. "The Duty of Waiting." *Biblical Illustrator,* Psalm 27:14.

[101] From *The Sunday School Times* cited by Cowper. *Streams in the Desert,* August 16.

[102] Simeon, C. *Horae Homileticae: Mark-Luke* (Vol. 12). (Holdsworth and Ball, 1832), 76.

[103] Dixon, Francis. *Great Questions in the New Testament, Series 56,* Study 2: "WHY COULDN'T WE DRIVE IT OUT?"

[104] https://www.preceptaustin.org/prayer_quotes, accessed June 15, 2022.

[105] Barclay, W., ed. *The Gospel of Mark.* (The Westminster John Knox Press, 1976), 219.

[106] https://www.christianquotes.info/quotes-by-topic/quotes-about-fasting/, accessed June 25, 2022.

[107] Wiersbe, W. W. *Wiersbe's Expository Outlines on the New Testament.* (Wheaton, IL: Victor Books, 1992), 125.

[108] Spurgeon, C. H. *Morning and Evening,* September 2.

[109] Henry, M. *Matthew Henry's Commentary on the Whole Bible: Complete and Unabridged in One Volume.* (Peabody: Hendrickson, 1994), 1713.

[110] Sproul, R. C., John Gerstner, and Arthur Lindsley, *Classical Apologetics,* 161.

[111] The Virgin Birth of Jesus. https://www.lwf.org/articles/the-virgin-birth-of-jesus, accessed July 1 2024.

[112] Criswell, W. A. *Criswell Study Bible,* 1 John 2: 2.

[113] Pink, A. W. *Exposition of the Gospel of John.* (Bible Truth Depot, 1923–1945), 362.

[114] Morgan, R. J. *Nelson's Annual Preacher's Sourcebook* (2002 Edition). (Nashville: Thomas Nelson Publishers, 2001), 183.

[115] Henry, M. *Matthew Henry's Commentary on the Whole Bible: Complete and Unabridged in One Volume.* (Peabody: Hendrickson, 1994), 1795.

[116] Criswell, W. A. *What To Do Until Jesus Comes Back.* (Nashville: Broadman Press, 1975), 44.

[117] Dixon, Francis. *Twelve Studies on the Life of Christ:* "The Certainty of His Return," No. 12 (August 24, 1974).

[118] http://www.jesusiscoming.com/Scripture.htm, accessed March 29, 2014.

Endnotes

[119] Henry, M. *Matthew Henry's Commentary on the Whole Bible: Complete and Unabridged in One Volume.* (Peabody: Hendrickson, 1994), 249.

[120] MacArthur, J., Jr. (Ed.). *The MacArthur Study Bible* (electronic ed.). (Nashville, TN: Word Pub., 1997), 265.

[121] Henry, M. *Matthew Henry's Commentary on the Whole Bible: Complete and Unabridged in One Volume.* (Peabody: Hendrickson, 1994), 249.

[122] Simeon, C. *Horae Homileticae: Numbers to Joshua* (Vol. 2). (Holdsworth and Ball, 1836), 326.

[123] Dixon, Francis. Bible Study Notes. "GREAT QUESTIONS IN THE OLD TESTAMENT," Series 55, Study #2.

[124] MacArthur, J., Jr. (Ed.). *The MacArthur Study Bible* (electronic ed.). (Nashville, TN: Word Pub., 1997), 1705.

[125] Ibid., 851.

[126] Gill, John. *Gill's Exposition of the Entire Bible,* Psalm 119:11.

[127] Spurgeon, C. H. *The Treasury of David: Psalms 111–119* (Vol. 5). (Marshall Brothers, n.d.), 157.

[128] Simeon, C. *Horae Homileticae: Psalms, LXXIII–CL* (Vol. 6). (London: Holdsworth and Ball, 1836), 305–306.

[129] *Benson Commentary,* Psalm 119:9.

[130] Henry, M. *Matthew Henry's Commentary on the Whole Bible: Complete and Unabridged in One Volume.* (Peabody: Hendrickson, 1994), 914.

[131] Spurgeon, C. H. *Morning and Evening,* April 14 (Evening).

[132] Spurgeon, C. H. "Understandest Thou What Thou Readest?" Sermon delivered May 11, 1884, Metropolitan Tabernacle.

[133] Henry, M. *Matthew Henry's Commentary on the Whole Bible: Complete and Unabridged in One Volume.* (Peabody: Hendrickson, 1994), 2099.

[134] Cited by Francis Dixon, *Twelve Studies on the Life of Christ:* "The Certainty of His Return," No. 12 (August 24, 1974).

[135] Criswell, W. A. *What To Do Until Jesus Comes Back.* (Nashville: Broadman Press, 1975), 17.

[136] Spurgeon, C. H. "The Heaven of Heaven." Sermon delivered August 9, 1868, Metropolitan Tabernacle.

[137] Henry, M. *Matthew Henry's Commentary on the Whole Bible: Complete and Unabridged in One Volume.* (Peabody: Hendrickson, 1994), 2276.

[138] *The Interpretation of St. Paul's First and Second Epistles to the Corinthians.* (Minneapolis: Augsburg, 1963), 744–45.

[139] Exell, J. S. *The Biblical Illustrator: I Corinthians,* (Vol. 1). (New York: Anson D. F. Randolph & Company), 533.

[140] Witmer, J. A. In J. F. Walvoord & R. B. Zuck (Eds.). *The Bible Knowledge Commentary: An Exposition of the Scriptures, Romans,* Vol. 2. (Wheaton, IL: Victor Books, 1985), 476.

[141] Ibid.

Endnotes

[142] Pfeiffer, C. F., & E. F. Harrison, eds. *The Wycliffe Bible Commentary: New Testament.* (Moody Press, 1962), Rom. 8:35.

[143] Spence-Jones, H. D. M. (Ed.). *The Pulpit Commentary: Romans.* (London; New York: Funk & Wagnalls Company, 1909), 254.

[144] Ibid.

[145] Spurgeon, C. H. "Love at Its Utmost." Sermon delivered September 11, 1887, Metropolitan Tabernacle.

[146] Mullins, E. Y. *Talks on Soul Winning.* (Nashville, TN: The Sunday School Board of the Southern Baptist Convention, 1920), 11.

[147] Leavell, Roland Q. *Evangelism, Christ's Imperative Command,* 4.

[148] Spence-Jones, H. D. M., ed. *St. John* (Vol. 1). (Funk & Wagnalls Company, 1909), 201.

[149] Criswell, W. A. "Divine Healing," (Sermon). James 5:14–15. July 25, 1965. https://wacriswell.com/sermons/1965/divine-healing-2/, accessed July 20, 2020.

[150] Vine, W. E., M. F. Unger & W. White, Jr. *Vine's Complete Expository Dictionary of Old and New Testament Words,* Vol. 2. (Nashville, TN: T. Nelson, 1996), 195.

[151] Barnes, Albert. *Notes on the Bible.* (1834), James 5:14.

[152] Swindoll, Chuck. *Swindoll's Living Insights New Testament Commentary: James, 1 & 2 Peter,* James 5:14–15.

[153] Ibid.

[154] Criswell, W. A. "Divine Healing," (Sermon). James 5:14–15. July 25, 1965. https:// wacriswell.com/sermons/1965/divine-healing-2/, accessed July 20, 2020.

[155] Lucado, Max. Tweet. Aug 4, 2016.

[156] Spurgeon, C. H. *Morning and Evening,* January 24 (Evening).

[157] Ibid.

[158] Unknown.

[159] Spurgeon, C. H. "Martha and Mary." Sermon delivered April 23, 1870, Metropolitan Tabernacle.

[160] Bounds, E. M. *Preacher and Prayer.* (Nashville: House of the M.E. Church, 1907), 30.

[161] Simeon, C. *Horae Homileticae: Genesis to Leviticus* (Vol. 1). (London: Holdsworth and Ball, 1836), 507.

[162] Spurgeon, C. H. "On Whose Side Are You?" Sermon delivered April 4, 1880, Metropolitan Tabernacle.

[163] Simeon, C. *Horae Homileticae: Genesis to Leviticus* (Vol. 1). (London: Holdsworth and Ball, 1836), 507.

[164] Exell, J. S. *The Biblical Illustrator: Joshua, Judges, and Ruth* (Vol. 1). (Chicago; Toronto: Fleming H. Revell Company; Francis Griffiths, 1909), 76.

Endnotes

[165] Spurgeon, C. H. "Watching for Christ's Coming." Sermon delivered April 7, 1889, Metropolitan Tabernacle.

[166] Exell, J. S. *The Biblical Illustrator: Joshua, Judges, and Ruth* (Vol. 1). (Chicago; Toronto: Fleming H. Revell Company; Francis Griffiths, 1909), 75.

[167] Henry, M. *Matthew Henry's Commentary on the Whole Bible: Complete and Unabridged in One Volume*. (Peabody: Hendrickson, 1994), 340.

[168] Hindson, E. E., & W. M. Kroll (Eds.). *KJV Bible Commentary*. (Nashville: Thomas Nelson, 1994), 474.

[169] Criswell, W. A., P. Patterson, E. R. Clendenen, D. L. Akin, M. Chamberlin, D. K. Patterson, & J. Pogue (Eds.). *Believer's Study Bible* (electronic ed.). (Nashville: Thomas Nelson, 1991), Jdg. 6:36–40.

[170] Exell, J. S. *The Biblical Illustrator: Joshua, Judges, and Ruth* (Vol. 2). (Chicago; Toronto: Fleming H. Revell Company; Francis Griffiths, 1909), 124.

[171] MacArthur, J., Jr. (Ed.). *The MacArthur Study Bible* (electronic ed.). (Nashville, TN: Word Pub., 1997), 345.

[172] Smith, J. E. *The Books of History*. (College Press, 1995), 155.

[173] Henry, M. *Matthew Henry's Commentary on the Whole Bible: Complete and Unabridged in One Volume*. (Peabody: Hendrickson, 1994), 456.

[174] Exell, J. S. *The Biblical Illustrator: 2 Samuel*. (New York; Chicago; Toronto: Fleming H. Revell Company; Francis Griffiths, 1909), 196.

[175] Criswell, W. A. & Paige Patterson. *Heaven*. (Wheaton, Ill: Tyndale House Publications, Inc., 1991), 34.

[176] Spence-Jones, H. D. M. (Ed.). *The Pulpit Commentary: 2 Samuel*. (London; New York: Funk & Wagnalls Company, 1909), 316.

[177] Henry, M. *Matthew Henry's Commentary on the Whole Bible: Complete and Unabridged in One Volume*. (Peabody: Hendrickson, 1994), 456.

[178] Lawson, George. *A Practical Exposition of the Book of Proverbs*, 1821.

[179] Bridges, Charles. 117.

[180] Henry, M., and T. Scott. *Matthew Henry's Concise Commentary*. (Oak Harbor, WA: Logos Research Systems, 1997), 1 Samuel 18:1–5.

[181] Carson, D. A. *The Gospel According to John*. (Inter-Varsity Press; W. B. Eerdmans, 1991), 491.

[182] Barclay, W., ed. *The Gospel of John* (Vol. 2). (Westminster John Knox Press, 1975), 158.

[183] Pink, A. W. *Exposition of the Gospel of John*. (Bible Truth Depot, 1923–1945), 762.

[184] MacArthur, J., Jr. (Ed.). *The MacArthur Study Bible* (electronic ed.). (Nashville, TN: Word Pub., 1997), 1713.

[185] Henry, M. *Matthew Henry's Commentary on the Whole Bible: Complete and Unabridged in One Volume*. (Peabody: Hendrickson, 1994), 1090.

[186] Spurgeon, C. H. "Preach the Gospel." Sermon delivered August 5, 1855, New Park Street Chapel.

Endnotes

[187] Henry, M. *Matthew Henry's Commentary on the Whole Bible: Complete and Unabridged in One Volume.* (Peabody: Hendrickson, 1994), 1090.

[188] Spurgeon, C. H. "The Shulamite's Choice Prayer." Sermon delivered February 25, 1861, Metropolitan Tabernacle.

[189] Spurgeon, Charles. *The Complete Works of C. H. Spurgeon, Volume 35: Sermons 2062–2120.* (Delmarva Publications, Inc., 2015), 873.

[190] "Does God Love Everyone?" https://www.lwf.org/who-is-god-what-is-he-like/does-god-love-me, accessed July 18, 2024.

[191] Spurgeon, C. H. "Immeasurable Love." Sermon delivered July 26th, 1885, Metropolitan Tabernacle.

[192] Henry, M. *Matthew Henry's Commentary on the Whole Bible: Complete and Unabridged in One Volume.* (Peabody: Hendrickson, 1994), 1460.

[193] Spurgeon. "Soul Winning." sermon delivered, 1869.

[194] Sanderson, Leonard. *Personal Soul Winning.* (Nashville: Convention Press, 1958), 7–8.

[195] Morgan, R. J. *Nelson's Annual Preacher's Sourcebook: 2002 Edition* (electronic ed.) (Nashville: Thomas Nelson Publishers, 2001), 40.

[196] www.vitalchristianity.org/docs/New%20Articles/Revivial-Requirement2.pdf, accessed May 10, 2014.

[197] Exell, J. S. *The Biblical Illustrator: The Psalms* (Vol. 3). (Fleming H. Revell Company; Francis Griffiths, 1909), 494.

[198] *Faith's Checkbook,* November 16.

[199] Ironside, H. A. *Notes on the Book of Proverbs.* (Neptune, NJ: Loizeaux Bros, 1908), 188.

[200] Bridges, C. *An Exposition of the Book of Proverbs.* (Robert Carter & Brothers, 1865), 491.

[201] MacArthur, J., Jr. (Ed.). *The MacArthur Study Bible* (electronic ed.). (Nashville, TN: Word Pub., 1997), 792.

[202] Maclaren, Alexander. *The Book of Psalms: Book II,* 177.

[203] Henry, Matthew. *Matthew Henry's Concise Bible Commentary,* Psalm 56:8.

[204] Boice, J. M. *Psalms 42–106: An Expositional Commentary.* (Grand Rapids, MI: Baker Books, 2005), 470.

[205] Barnes, Albert. *Notes on the Bible.* (1834), Psalm 56:8.

[206] Spence-Jones, H. D. M., ed. *Psalms* (Vol. 2). (Funk & Wagnalls Company, 1909), 5.

[207] Henry, M. *Matthew Henry's Commentary on the Whole Bible: Complete and Unabridged in One Volume.* (Peabody: Hendrickson, 1994), 876.

[208] Ibid., 2313.

[209] Ironside, H. A. *Notes on the Book of Proverbs.* (Neptune, NJ: Loizeaux Bros, 1908), 437.

[210] MacArthur, J. F., Jr. *Ephesians.* (Moody Press, 1986), 138.

[211] Spurgeon, C. H. "The Ascension of Christ." Sermon delivered March 25, 1871, Metropolitan Tabernacle.
[212] Exell, J. S. *Proverbs.* (Fleming H. Revell Company, n.d.), 689.
[213] Ibid., 687.
[214] Ibid., 688.
[215] Bridges, C. *An Exposition of the Book of Proverbs.* (Robert Carter & Brothers, 1865), 527.
[216] Exell, J. S. *The Biblical Illustrator: Leviticus and Numbers* (Vol. 1). (New York: Anson D. F. Randolph & Company), 107.
[217] Symington, Andrew James. *Thomas Guthrie: A Biographical Sketch.* (London: Houlston & Sons, 1879), 153.
[218] Exell, J. S. *The Biblical Illustrator: Leviticus and Numbers* (Vol. 1). (New York: Anson D. F. Randolph & Company), 106.
[219] Spurgeon, C. H. *The Soulwinner.* (New Kensington, PA: Whitaker House, 1995), 253.
[220] Spurgeon, C. H. "TO YOU." Sermon Delivered July 9, 1876, Metropolitan Tabernacle.
[221] Barclay, W., ed. *The Gospel of Mark.* (The Westminster John Knox Press, 1976), 290.
[222] Wessel, W. W. in F. E. Gaebelein (Ed.), *The Expositor's Bible Commentary: Matthew, Mark, Luke* (Vol. 8). (Grand Rapids, MI: Zondervan Publishing House, 1984), 736.
[223] McGee, J. V. *Thru the Bible Commentary: The Gospels* (Mark), (electronic ed., Vol. 36). (Nashville: Thomas Nelson, 1991), (electronic ed., Vol. 36). (Nashville: Thomas Nelson, 1991), 147.
[224] Hobbs, H. H. *My Favorite Illustrations.* (Nashville, TN: Broadman Press, 1990), 133.
[225] Criswell. "What I Believe About Heaven: The Inexpressible Preciousness." Sermon delivered June 24, 1990, First Baptist Church, Dallas, Texas.
[226] Wiersbe, W. W. Wiersbe's Expository Outlines on the New Testament. (Wheaton, IL: Victor Books, 1992), 133.
[227] Criswell, W. A., P. Patterson, E. R. Clendenen, D. L. Akin, M. Chamberlin, D. K. Patterson, & J. Pogue (Eds.). *Believer's Study Bible* (electronic ed.). (Nashville: Thomas Nelson, 1991), Mt. 19:9.
[228] Adrian Rogers. "A Word with You," Apr. 8, 2014. http://www.lightsource.com, accessed July 5, 2014.
[229] Balz, H. R., & Schneider, G. *Exegetical Dictionary of the New Testament* (Vol. 3). (Eerdmans, 1990), 43.
[230] Cited in Swindoll, Chuck. *Paul: A Man of Grace and Grit.* (Nashville: Word Publishing, 2002), 176.
[231] MacArthur, J. F., Jr. *Acts* (Vol. 2). (Moody Press, 1994), 82.

Endnotes

[232] Henry, M. *Matthew Henry's Commentary on the Whole Bible: Complete and Unabridged in One Volume.* (Peabody: Hendrickson, 1994), 2133.

[233] Cited in Swindoll, Chuck. *Paul: A Man of Grace and Grit.* (Nashville: Word Publishing, 2002), 176.

[234] Exell, J. S. *The Biblical Illustrator: Acts* (Vol. 15). (Grand Rapids: Baker Book House, undated), 450.

[235] Henry, M. *Matthew Henry's Commentary on the Whole Bible: Complete and Unabridged in One Volume.* (Peabody: Hendrickson, 1994), 2133.

[236] Ibid, 291.

[237] Exell, J. S. *The Biblical Illustrator: Acts* (Vol. 15). (Grand Rapids: Baker Book House, undated), 452.

[238] Exell, J. S. *The Biblical Illustrator: The Psalms* (Vol. 5). (Fleming H. Revell Company; Francis Griffiths, 1909), 285.

[239] Spurgeon, C. H. *Morning and Evening,* May 30 (Morning).

[240] Spurgeon, C. H. "Purging Out the Leaven." Sermon delivered December 11, 1870, Metropolitan Tabernacle.

[241] Wiersbe, W. W. *Wiersbe's Expository Outlines on the Old Testament.* (Wheaton, IL: Victor Books, 1993), Pr 18:13.

[242] Henry, M. *Matthew Henry's Commentary on the Whole Bible: Complete and Unabridged in One Volume.* (Peabody: Hendrickson, 1994), 995.

[243] Wiersbe, W. W. *Wiersbe's Expository Outlines on the Old Testament.* (Wheaton, IL: Victor Books, 1993), Pr 18:13.

[244] Ironside, H. A. *Notes on the Book of Proverbs.* (Neptune, NJ: Loizeaux Bros, 1908), 232.

[245] Spence-Jones, H. D. M., ed. *Proverbs.* (Funk & Wagnalls Company, 1909), 354.

[246] Henry, M. *Matthew Henry's Commentary on the Whole Bible: Complete and Unabridged in One Volume.* (Peabody: Hendrickson, 1994), 413.

[247] Spurgeon, C. H. "David's First Victory." Sermon published December 8, 1904.

[248] "Live Like a King in Victory," November 1, 2021.

[249] Henry, M. *Matthew Henry's Commentary on the Whole Bible: Complete and Unabridged in One Volume.* (Peabody: Hendrickson, 1994), 414.

[250] Wiersbe, W. W. *Wiersbe's Expository Outlines on the Old Testament.* (Wheaton, IL: Victor Books, 1993), 1 Sa 17.

[251] Ibid.

[252] Spurgeon, C. H. "A Plain Man's Sermon," (sermon #1879).

[253] http://defendingcontending.com, March 30, 2014.

[254] Spurgeon, C. H. "A Preacher from the Dead." Sermon delivered July 26, 1857, at the Music Hall, Surrey Gardens.

[255] Sproul, R. C. "The New Genesis: The Holy Spirit and Regeneration." www.the-highway.com/genesis_Sproul.html, accessed May 21, 2010.

Endnotes

[256] Henry, M. *Matthew Henry's Commentary on the Whole Bible: Complete and Unabridged in One Volume.* (Peabody: Hendrickson, 1994), 2064.

[257] Ibid.

[258] Chadwick, George Alexander on the ascension of Jesus [G. A. Chadwick was a 19–20th century bishop].

[259] Exell, J. S. The Biblical Illustrator (Acts): Or Anecdotes, Similes, Emblems, Illustrations; Expository, Scientific, Geographical, Historical, and Homiletic, Gathered from a Wide Range of Home and Foreign Literature, on the Verses of the Bible. (Logos Research Systems, Inc., 1997), 73.

[260] Gill, John. *A Body of Doctrinal Divinity,* Book Five.

[261] Hayford, J. W. (Ed.). *Spirit-Filled Life Study Bible* (electronic ed.). (Nashville, TN: Thomas Nelson, 1997), Hebrews 1:7.

[262] Ibid.

[263] MacDonald, W. *Believer's Bible Commentary: Old and New Testaments.* (A. Farstad, Ed.) (Nashville: Thomas Nelson, 1995), 2161.

[264] Spence-Jones, H. D. M. (Ed.). *The Pulpit Commentary: Hebrews.* (London; New York: Funk & Wagnalls Company, 1909), 30.

[265] Ibid.

[266] Jeremiah, David. "Your Heavenly Escorts," Turning Point. https://www.oneplace.com/ ministries/turning-point/read/articles/your-Heavenly-escorts-16251.html, accessed March 30, 2020.

[267] Spurgeon, C. H. Morning and Evening. (Grand Rapids: Zondervan Publishing House, 1969), October 3.

[268] Exell, J. S. *The Biblical Illustrator: Hebrews* (Vol. 1). (London: James Nisbet & Co, 1909), 64.

[269] Bunyan, J. *Bunyan's Dying Sayings* (Vol. 1). (Bellingham, WA: Logos Bible Software, 2006), 66.

[270] "Start Right: Believer's Baptism." October 4, 2022. https://www.lwf.org/sermons/audio/start-right-believers-baptism-1736, accessed July 29, 2024.

[271] Mosheim, J. L. 1959. Ecclesiastical History (Vol. I). (Rosemead, CA: Old Paths Book Club), 36.

[272] Craigie, P. C. *Psalms 1–50* (Vol. 19). (Dallas: Word, Incorporated, 1998), 108.

[273] Spurgeon, C. H. *The Treasury of David: Psalms 120–150* (Vol. 6). (Marshall Brothers, n.d.), Psalm 144:3.

[274] Henry, M. *Matthew Henry's Commentary on the Whole Bible: Complete and Unabridged in One Volume.* (Peabody: Hendrickson, 1994), 754.

[275] Lloyd-Jones, D. M. "The Great Conflict." In *Courageous Christianity* (1st U.S. ed., Vol. 2). (Crossway Books, 2001), 273.

[276] Ibid.

[277] www.bartleby.com, John Bartlett (1820–1905). Familiar Quotations, 10th ed. 1919.

Endnotes

[278] Exell, J. S. *The Biblical Illustrator: Jeremiah* (Vol. 1). (Fleming H. Revell Company; Francis Griffiths, 1905), 276.

[279] The author is indebted to D. Johnston for the reasons cited for the wicked's prosperity, adapted. "The Reasons Why the Wicked Are Permitted to Prosper," J. S. Exell. *The Biblical Illustrator: Jeremiah* (Vol. 1). (Fleming H. Revell Company; Francis Griffiths, 1905), 275.

[280] Exell, J. S. *The Biblical Illustrator: Jeremiah* (Vol. 1). (Fleming H. Revell Company; Francis Griffiths, 1905), 275.

[281] Spence-Jones, H. D. M. (Ed.). *The Pulpit Commentary: Psalms* (Vol. 2). (London; New York: Funk & Wagnalls Company, 1909), 72.

[282] *Benson Commentary,* Psalm 73:18.

[283] Hamilton, William W. *Sermons on the Books of the Bible* (Vol. 3), 258.

[284] https://www.christianquotes.info/top-quotes/22-powerful-quotes-overcoming-fear/, accessed November 12, 2020.

[285] Perowne, J. J. S. *The Book of Psalms: A New Translation, With Introductions and Notes, Explanatory and Critical* (Fifth Edition, Revised, Vol. 1). (London; Cambridge: George Bell and Sons; Deighton Bell and Co, 1883), 275.

[286] Barnes, Albert. *Barnes Notes on the Bible,* Psalm 27:1.

[287] Ibid.

[288] Derickson, G. W. *First, Second, and Third John,* (House, H. W., W. H. Harris III, & A. W. Pitts, [eds.]) (Bellingham, WA: Lexham Press, 2012), 467.

[289] Rogers, Adrian. "Facing Your Fear." May 14, 2013. https://www.lwf.org/articles/facing-your-fear, accessed November 12, 2020.

[290] https://www.christianquotes.info/top-quotes/22-powerful-quotes-overcoming-fear/, accessed November 12, 2020.

[291] "Christian Quotes on Fear," dailychristianquote.com/dcqfear.html, accessed December 1, 2011.

[292] Ibid.

[293] Spurgeon, C. H. *Morning and Evening.* (London: Passmore & Alabaster), June 16 (Evening).

[294] Exell, J. S. *The Biblical Illustrator: Jude.* (James Nisbet & Co.), 87.

[295] Spurgeon, *An All-Round Ministry,* 33.

[296] Morgan, R. J. *Nelson's Annual Preacher's Sourcebook* (2002 Edition). (Nashville: Thomas Nelson Publishers, 2001), 232.

[297] Stalker, J. *The Seven Deadly Sins.* (London: Hodder and Stoughton, 1901), 80.

[298] Exell, J. S. *Proverbs.* (Fleming H. Revell Company, n.d.), 629.

[299] Lawson, G. *Exposition of the Book of Proverbs* (Vol. 1). (David Brown; W. Oliphant; F. Pillans; M. Ogle; Ogle, Duncan, and Co.; J. Nisbet, 1821), 308.

[300] Ironside, H. A. *Notes on the Book of Proverbs.* (Neptune, NJ: Loizeaux Bros, 1908), 70.

Endnotes

[301] Criswell, W. A., P. Patterson, E. R. Clendenen, D. L. Akin, M. Chamberlin, D. K. Patterson, & J. Pogue (Eds.). *Believer's Study Bible* (electronic ed.). (Nashville: Thomas Nelson, 1991), Pr 5:19.
[302] Bridges, C. *An Exposition of the Book of Proverbs.* (Robert Carter & Brothers, 1865), 287.
[303] Ironside, H. A. *Notes on the Book of Proverbs.* (Neptune, NJ: Loizeaux Bros, 1908), 264.
[304] Spurgeon, C. H. "The Covenant." Sermon published August 3, 1911. Delivered at Metropolitan Tabernacle.
[305] Henry, M. *Matthew Henry's Commentary on the Whole Bible: Complete and Unabridged in One Volume.* (Peabody: Hendrickson, 1994), 999.
[306] Hindson, E. E., & W. M. Kroll (Eds.). *KJV Bible Commentary.* (Nashville: Thomas Nelson, 1994), 2253.
[307] Henry, M. *Matthew Henry's Commentary on the Whole Bible: Complete and Unabridged in One Volume.* (Peabody: Hendrickson, 1994), 1806.
[308] MacDonald, W. *Believer's Bible Commentary: Old and New Testaments.* (A. Farstad, Ed.) (Nashville: Thomas Nelson, 1995), 1353.
[309] Henry, M. *Matthew Henry's Commentary on the Whole Bible: Complete and Unabridged in One Volume.* (Peabody: Hendrickson, 1994), 2285.
[310] Spence-Jones, H. D. M., ed. *Obadiah.* (Funk & Wagnalls Company, 1909), 9.
[311] Rogers, Adrian. "An Unchanging Message to a Changing World," sermon.
[312] Henry, M. *Matthew Henry's Commentary on the Whole Bible: Complete and Unabridged in One Volume.* (Peabody: Hendrickson, 1994), 1521.
[313] Courson, J. *Jon Courson's Application Commentary.* (Thomas Nelson, 2003), 1123.
[314] Spence-Jones, H. D. M., ed. *Amos.* (Funk & Wagnalls Company, 1909), 182.
[315] MacArthur, J., Jr. (Ed.). *The MacArthur Study Bible* (electronic ed.). (Nashville, TN: Word Pub., 1997), 1773.
[316] Exell, J. S. *The Biblical Illustrator: Second Corinthians* (Fleming H. Revell Company, n.d.), 345.
[317] Simeon, C. *Horae Homileticae: Hosea to Malachi* (Vol. 10). (London: Holdsworth and Ball, 1832), 325.
[318] Fausset, A. R. "Jeremiah–Malachi," in P. Jamieson, A. R. Fausset, and D. Brown. *A Commentary Critical, Experimental and Practical on the Old and New Testaments,* 6 vols. (Grand Rapids: Eerdmans, 1967), 4:606.
[319] Wiersbe, W. W. *Wiersbe's Expository Outlines on the New Testament.* (Wheaton, IL: Victor Books, 1992), 455.
[320] Exell, J. S. *The Biblical Illustrator: Galatians.* (Fleming H. Revell Company, n.d.), 29.
[321] Spurgeon, C. H. *The Sword and Trowel,* April 1887, 196.
[322] Exell, J. S. *Isaiah* (Vol. 1). (Fleming H. Revell Company, n.d.), 133.

Endnotes

[323] Bridges, C. *An Exposition of the Book of Proverbs.* (Robert Carter & Brothers, 1865), 388.

[324] Spurgeon, C. H. "Concealing the Words of God." Sermon delivered APRIL 27, 1879. Metropolitan Tabernacle.

[325] MacArthur, J. *1 Corinthians: Godly Solutions for Church Problems.* (W Publishing Group, 2001), 59.

[326] Simeon, C. *Horae Homileticae: Galatians-Ephesians* (Vol. 17). (London: Holdsworth and Ball, 1833), 20.

[327] Interview with John Piper. "If God Never Leaves Me, Why Does He Withdraw?" https://www.desiringgod.org/interviews/if-god-never-leaves-me-why-does-he-withdraw, accessed August 4, 2024.

[328] Spurgeon, C. H. *Psalms.* (Crossway Books, 1993), 28–29.

[329] Three of the four headings only adapted from Spurgeon, C. H. "The Sinner's Only Alternative." Sermon delivered December 27, 1861, Metropolitan Tabernacle.

[330] Wiersbe, W. W. *With the Word Bible Commentary.* (Thomas Nelson, 1991), 2 Ki 7.

[331] Exell, J. S. *The Biblical Illustrator: Job.* (Fleming H. Revell Company; Francis Griffiths, 1909), 339.

[332] *First Presbyterian Magazine,* Vol. LVI.-No. 5. (34-36 Cadogan Street, Glasgow: N. Adshead & Son, September, 1951).

[333] Spurgeon, C. H. "God Is With Us." Sermon delivered July 17, 1864, Metropolitan Tabernacle.

[334] Rogers, Adrian. "Let the Fire Fall," sermon preached January 14, 1990.

[335] Spurgeon, C. H. "God Is With Us." Sermon delivered July 17, 1864, Metropolitan Tabernacle.

[336] Spurgeon, C. H. "The Great Sin of Doing Nothing." Sermon delivered August 5, 1886, Metropolitan Tabernacle.

[337] Henry, M. *Matthew Henry's Commentary on the Whole Bible: Complete and Unabridged in One Volume.* (Peabody: Hendrickson, 1994), 233.

[338] Wiersbe, W. W. *With the Word Bible Commentary.* (Thomas Nelson, 1991), Nu 32.

[339] Henry, M. *Matthew Henry's Commentary on the Whole Bible: Complete and Unabridged in One Volume.* (Peabody: Hendrickson, 1994), 1233.

[340] Ibid., 969.

[341] Ibid., 2255.

[342] Clarke, Adam. *Commentary on the Bible.* (1831), 1 Corinthians 15:44.

[343] Courson, J. *Jon Courson's Application Commentary.* (Thomas Nelson, 2003), 1090.

[344] Wiersbe, W. W. *Wiersbe's Expository Outlines on the New Testament.* (Wheaton, IL: Victor Books, 1992), 467.

[345] MacDonald, W. *Believer's Bible Commentary: Old and New Testaments.* (A. Farstad, Ed.) (Nashville: Thomas Nelson, 1995), 1353.
[346] Clarke, Adam. *Commentary on the Bible.* (1831), 1 Corinthians 15:44.

www.ingramcontent.com/pod-product-compliance
Lightning Source LLC
Chambersburg PA
CBHW070755100426
42742CB00012B/2137